51 Large Print Dot to Dot Book

Enjoy connecting the dots of beautiful scenes

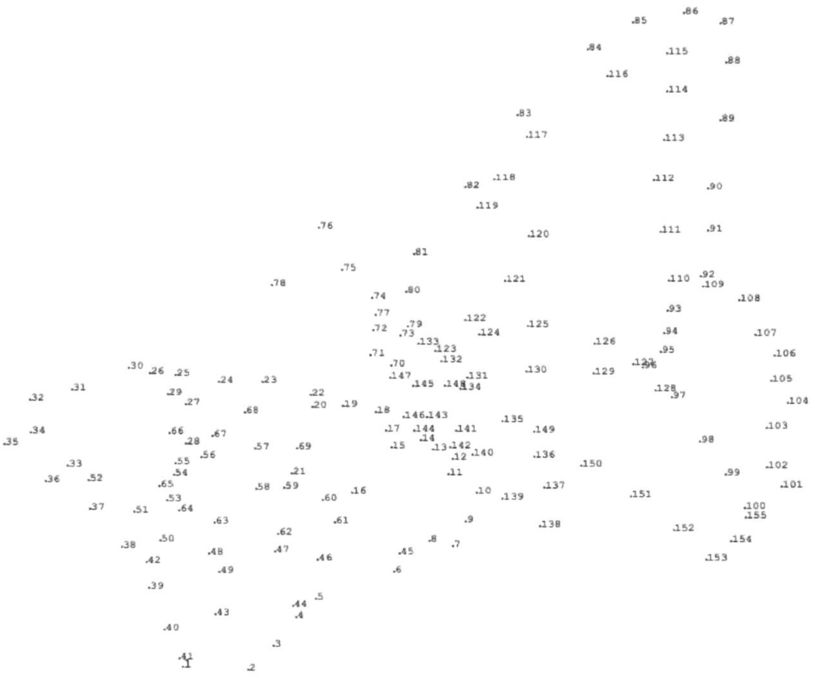

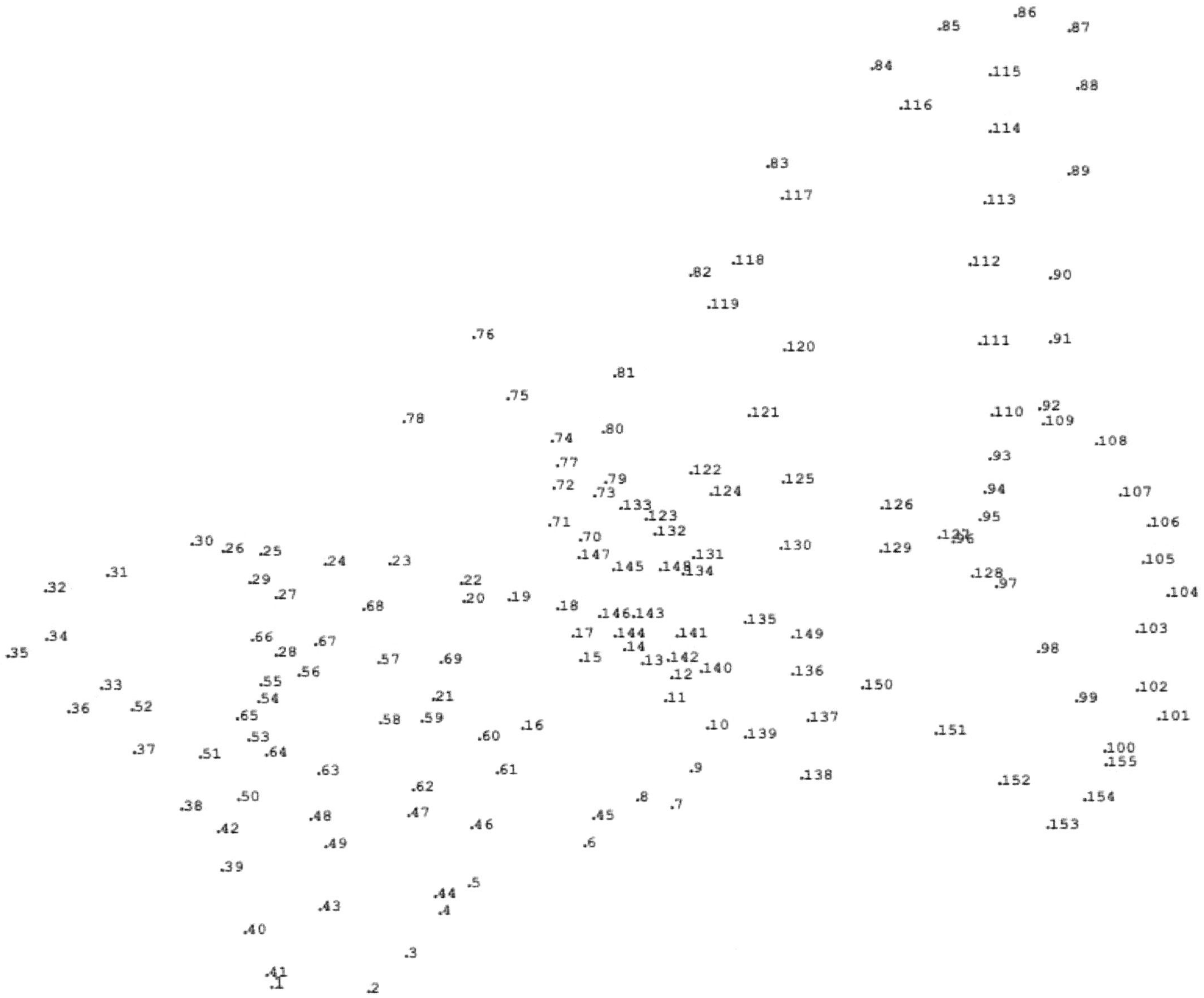

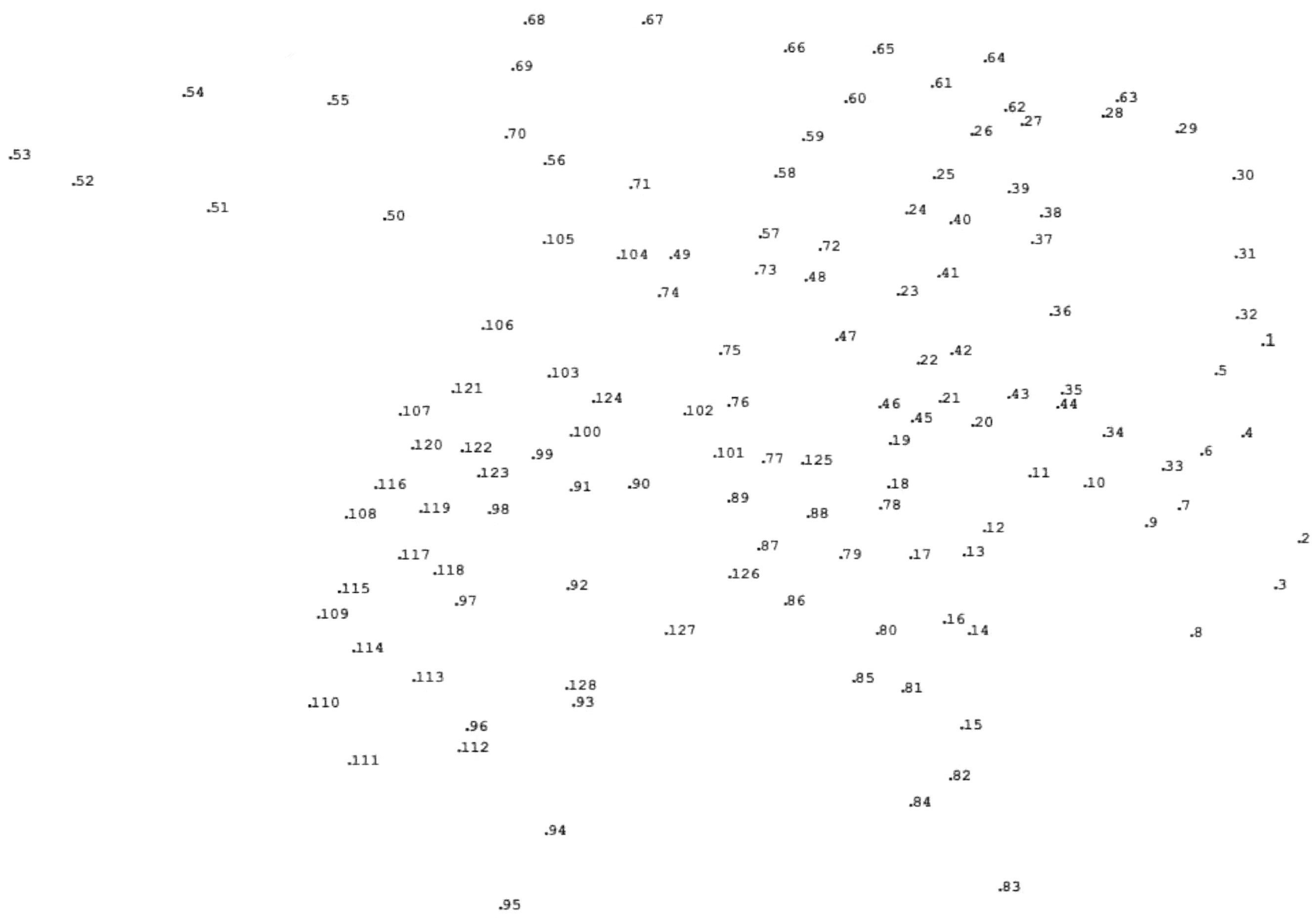
.1
.2
.3
.4
.5
.6
.7
.8
.9
.10
.11
.12
.13
.14
.15
.16
.17
.18
.19
.20
.21
.22
.23
.24
.25
.26
.27
.28
.29
.30
.31
.32
.33
.34
.35
.36
.37
.38
.39
.40
.41
.42
.43
.44
.45
.46
.47
.48
.49
.50
.51
.52
.53
.54
.55
.56
.57
.58
.59
.60
.61
.62
.63
.64
.65
.66
.67
.68
.69
.70
.71
.72
.73
.74
.75
.76
.77
.78
.79
.80
.81
.82
.83
.84
.85
.86
.87
.88
.89
.90
.91
.92
.93
.94
.95
.96
.97
.98
.99
.100
.101
.102
.103
.104
.105
.106
.107
.108
.109
.110
.111
.112
.113
.114
.115
.116
.117
.118
.119
.120
.121
.122
.123
.124
.125
.126
.127
.128

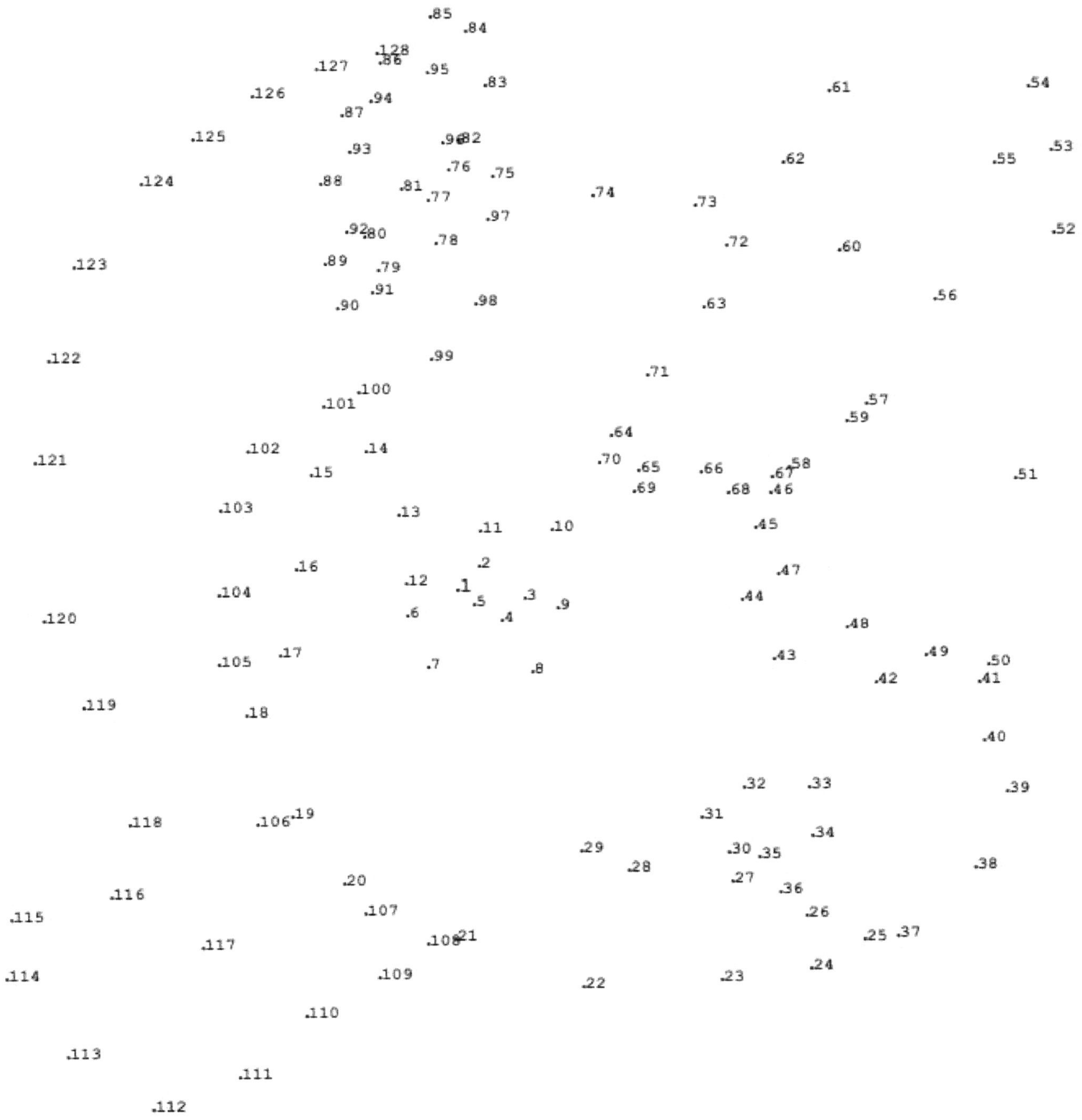

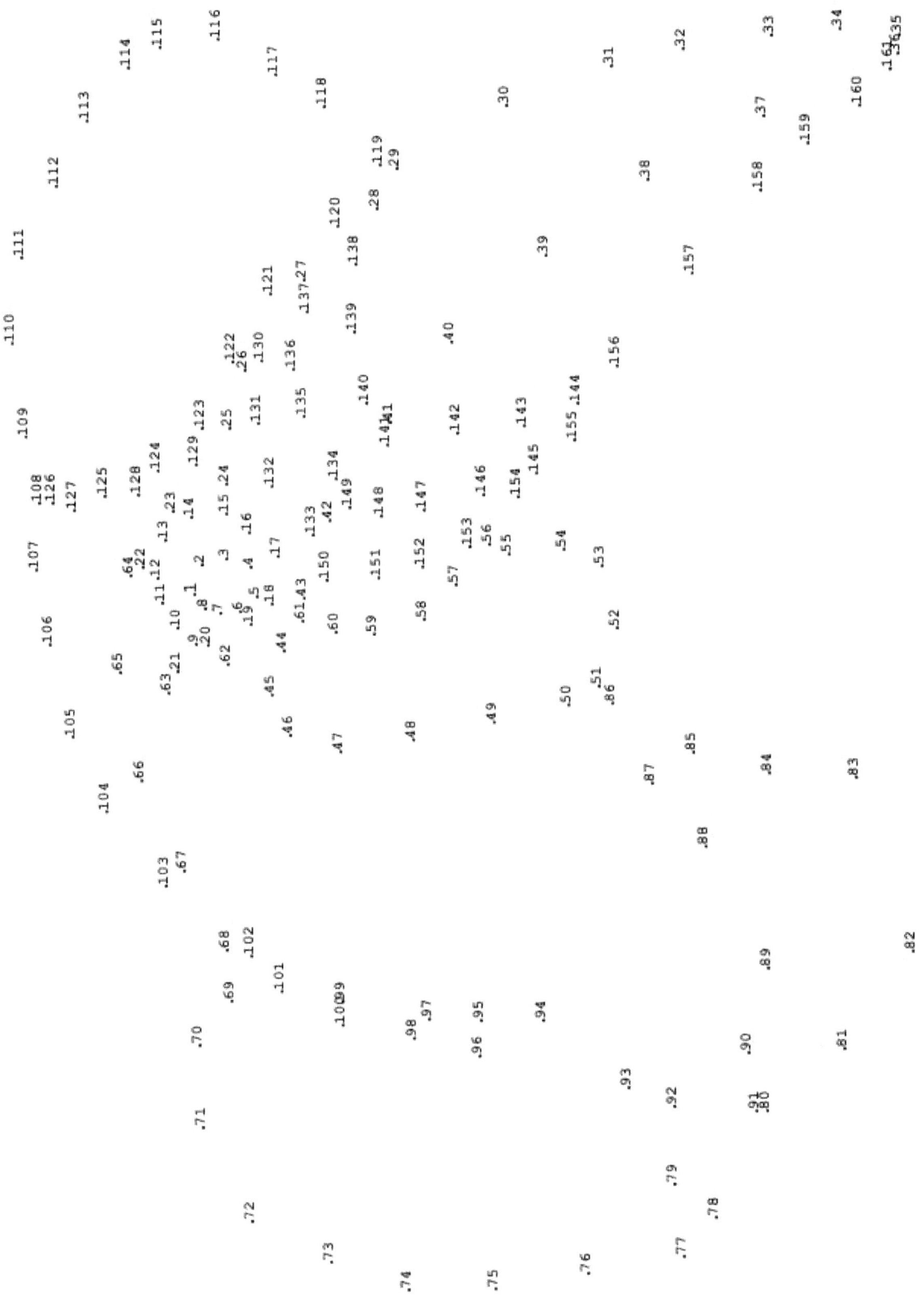

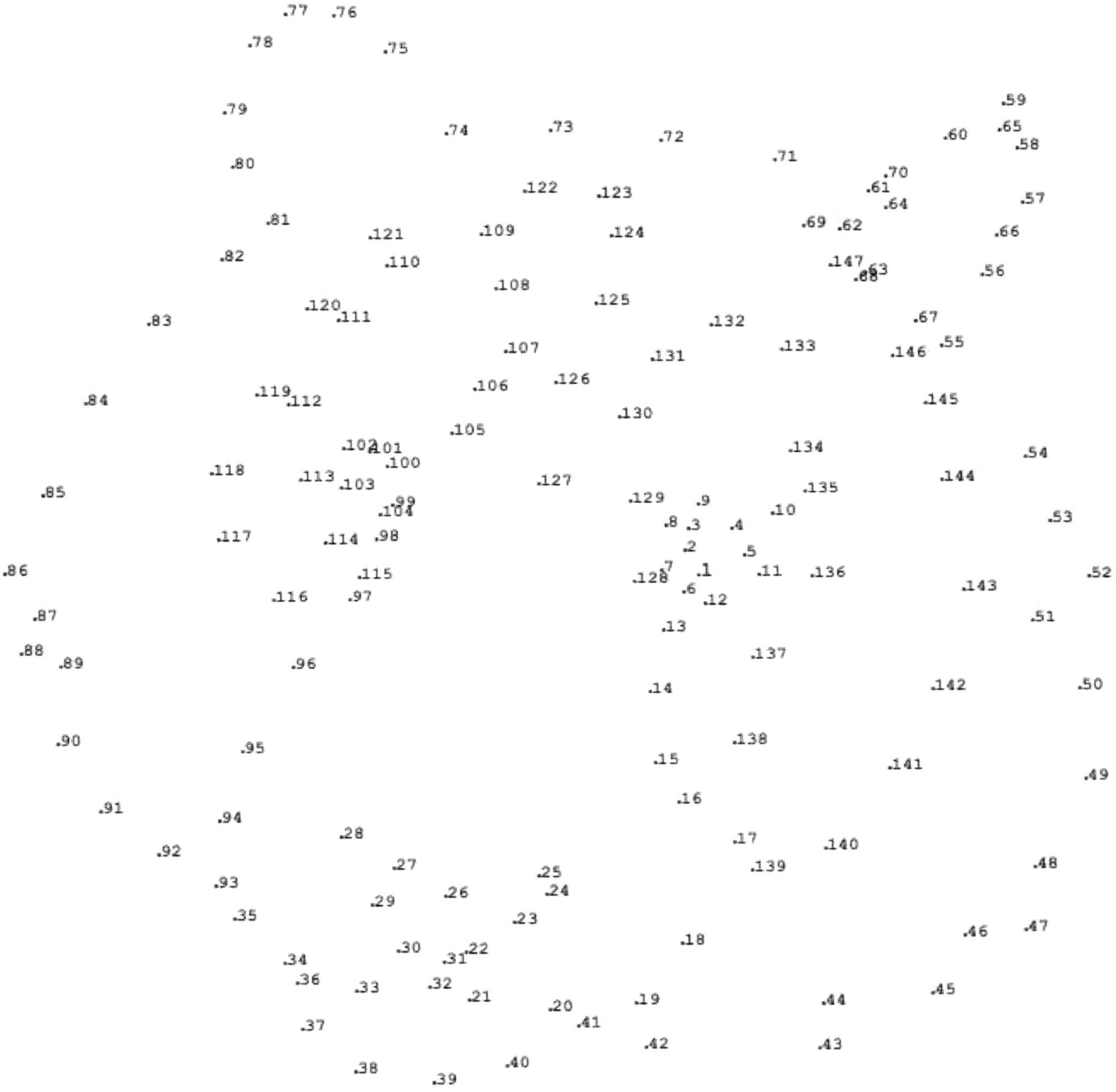

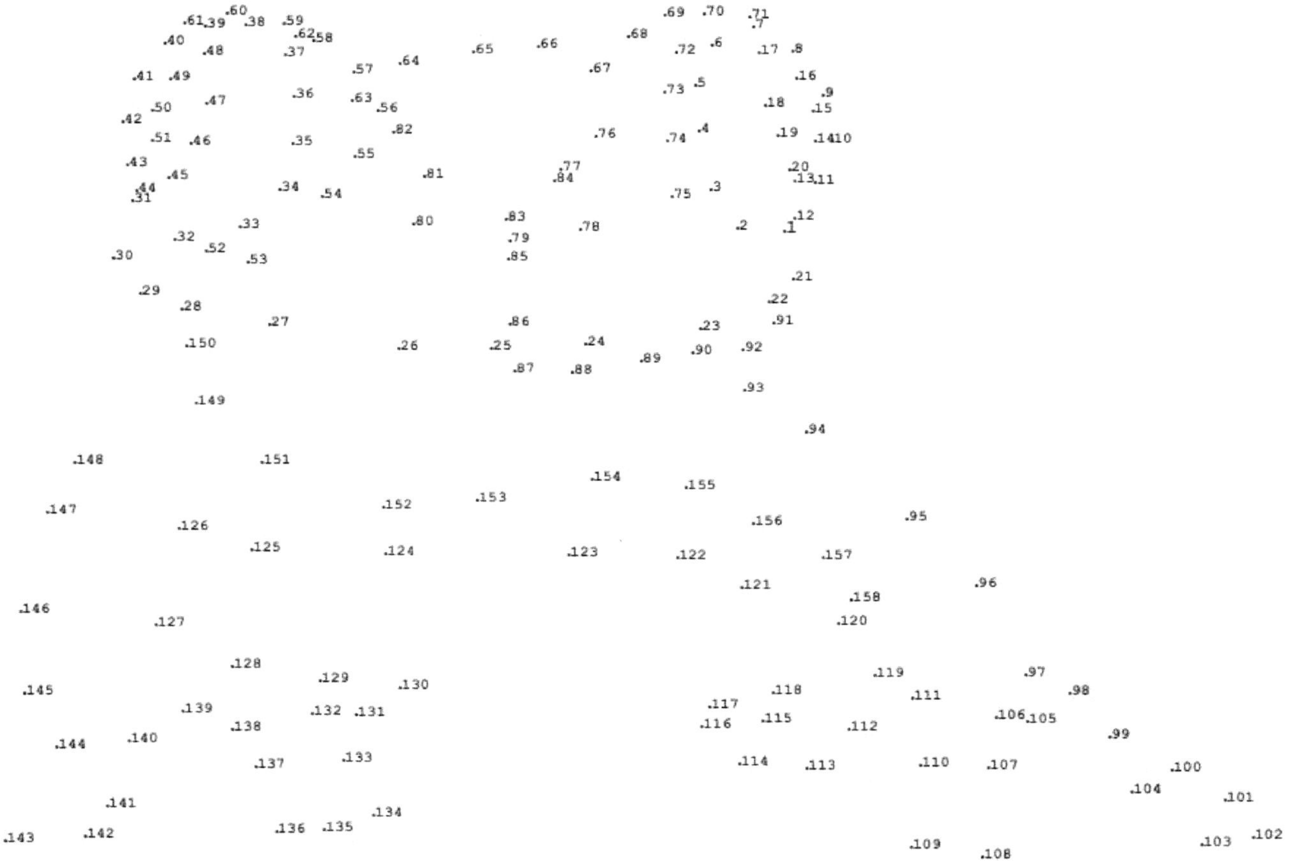

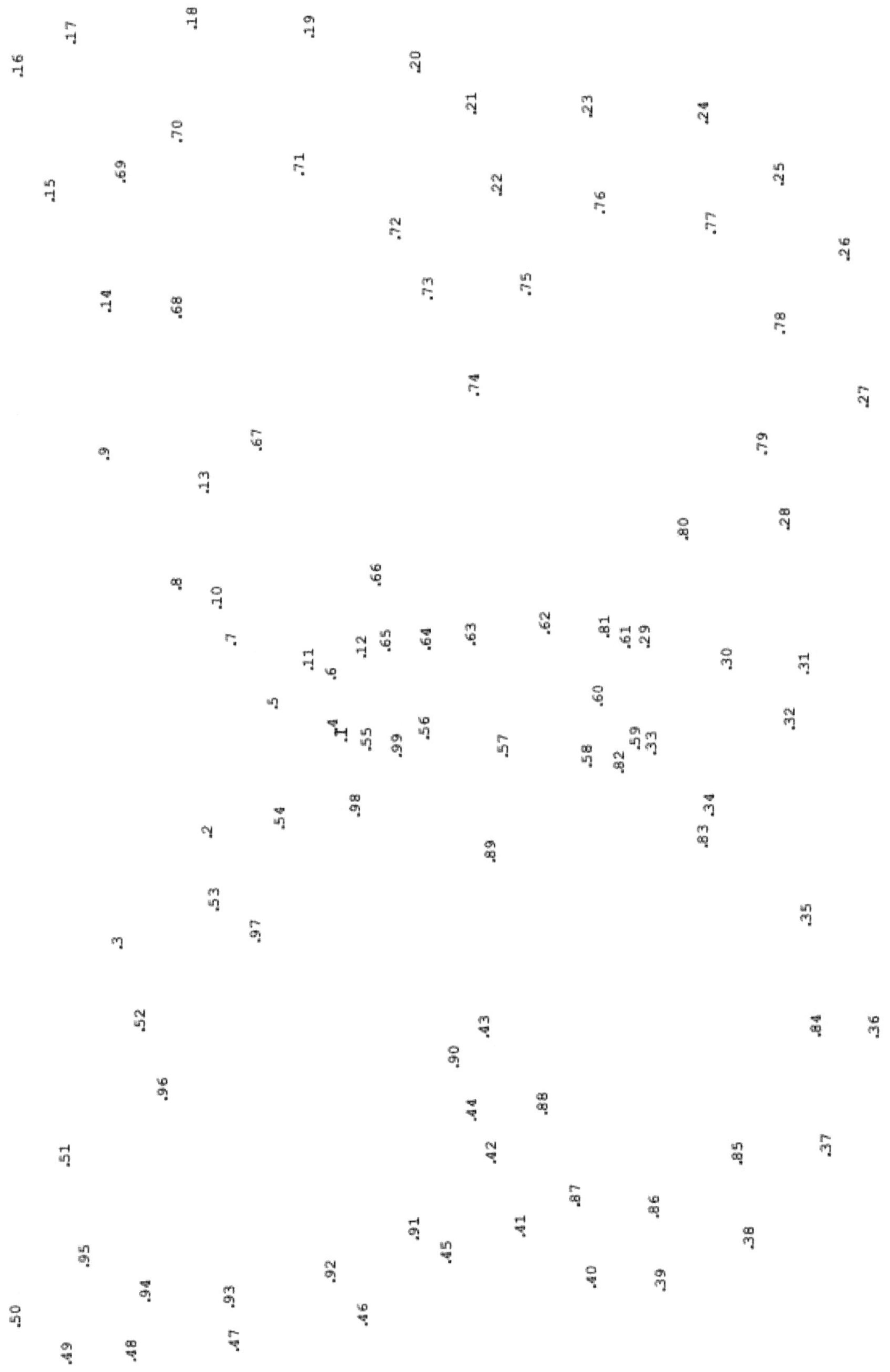

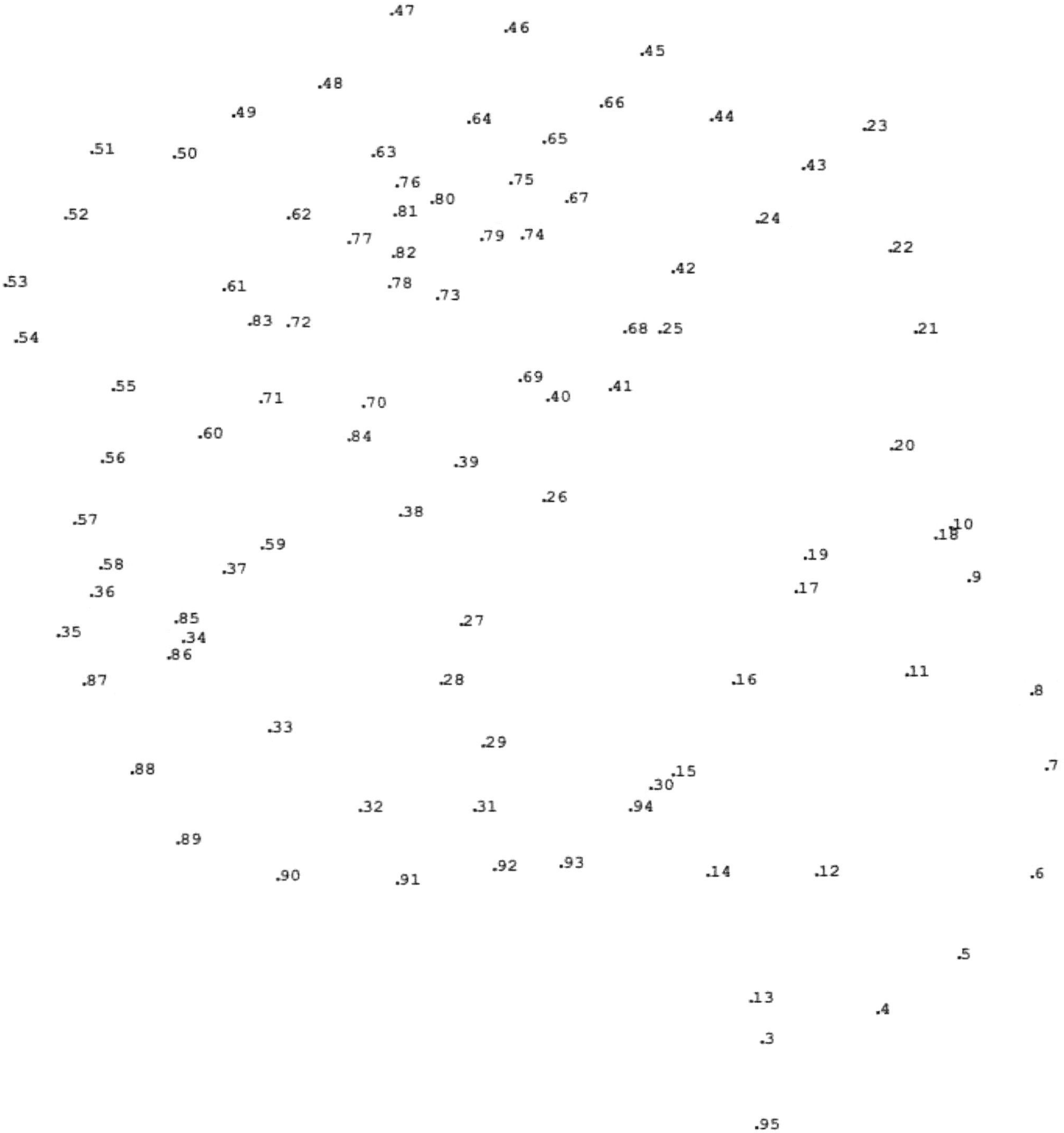

3
4
5
6
7
8
9
10
11
12
13
14
15
16
17
18
19
20
21
22
23
24
25
26
27
28
29
30
31
32
33
34
35
36
37
38
39
40
41
42
43
44
45
46
47
48
49
50
51
52
53
54
55
56
57
58
59
60
61
62
63
64
65
66
67
68
69
70
71
72
73
74
75
76
77
78
79
80
81
82
83
84
85
86
87
88
89
90
91
92
93
94
95

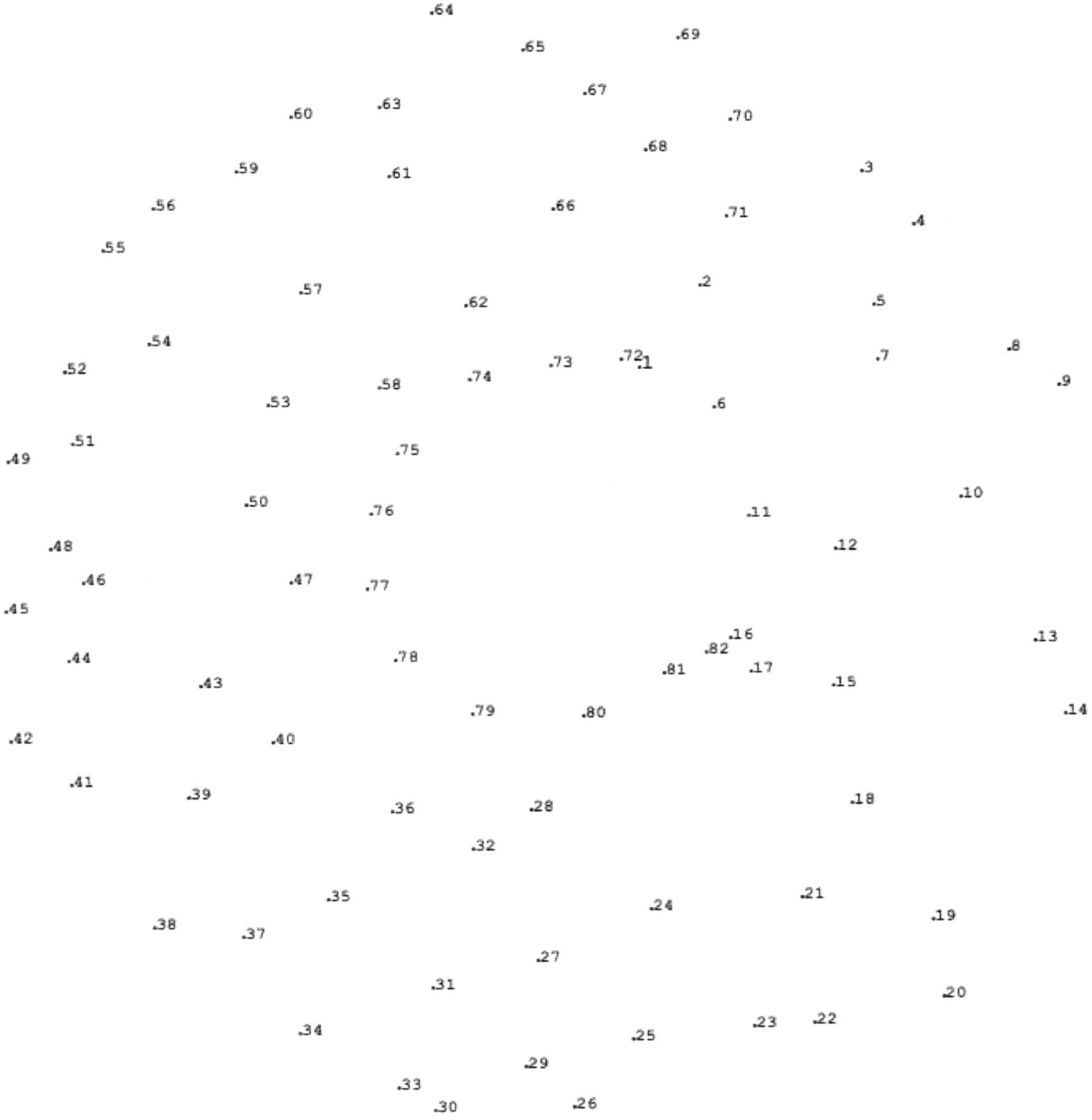
.64
.65
.69
.67
.60
.63
.70
.68
.59
.61
.3
.56
.66
.71
.4
.55
.57
.62
.2
.5
.54
.8
.52
.73
.72
.1
.74
.7
.58
.9
.53
.6
.51
.49
.75
.10
.50
.76
.11
.48
.12
.46
.47
.77
.45
.16
.82
.13
.44
.78
.81
.17
.15
.43
.79
.80
.14
.42
.40
.41
.39
.36
.28
.18
.32
.35
.21
.24
.19
.38
.37
.27
.31
.20
.23
.22
.34
.25
.29
.33
.30
.26

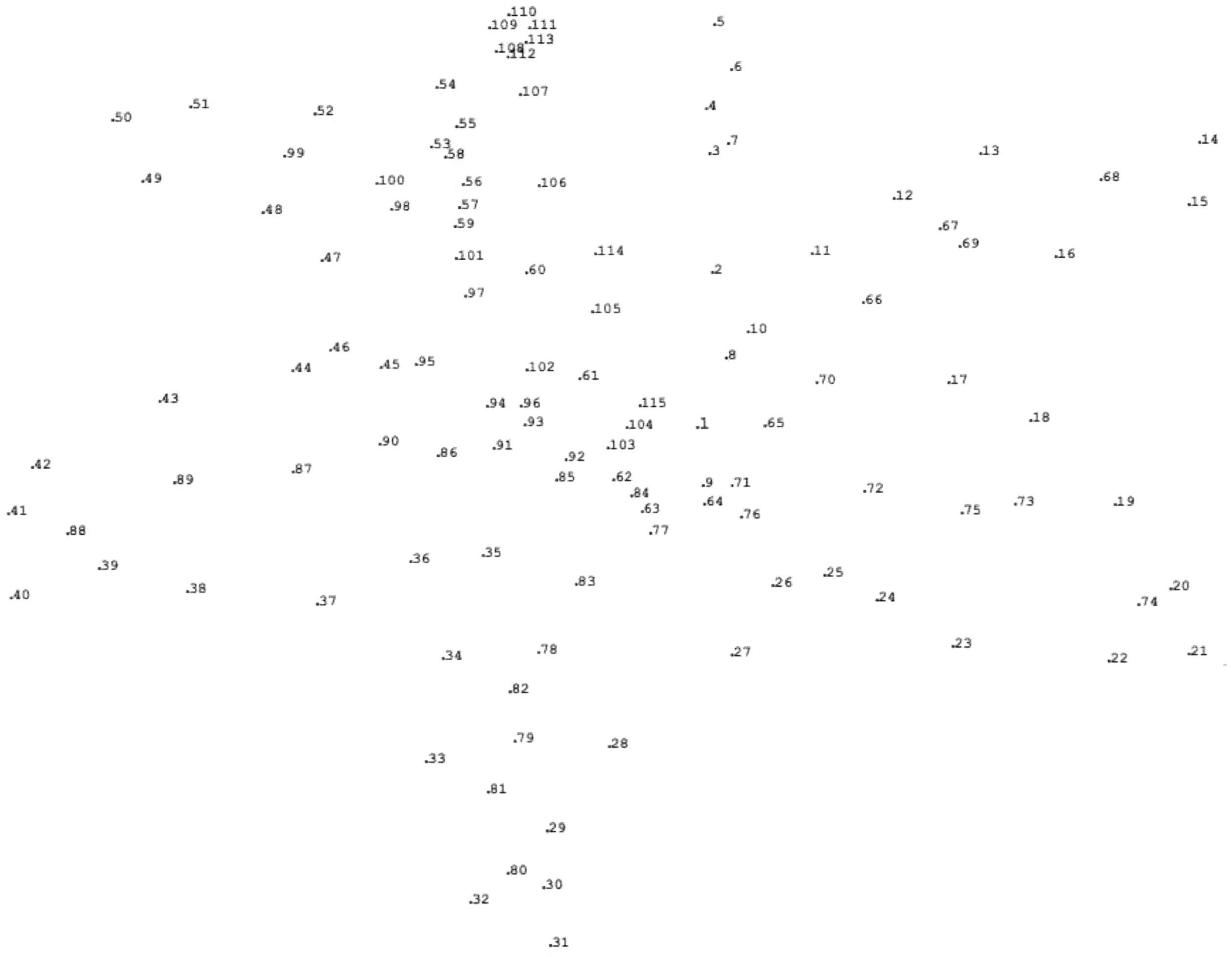

.1
.2
.3
.4
.5
.6
.7
.8
.9
.10
.11
.12
.13
.14
.15
.16
.17
.18
.19
.20
.21
.22
.23
.24
.25
.26
.27
.28
.29
.30
.31
.32
.33
.34
.35
.36
.37
.38
.39
.40
.41
.42
.43
.44
.45
.46
.47
.48
.49
.50
.51
.52
.53
.54
.55
.56
.57
.58
.59
.60
.61
.62
.63
.64
.65
.66
.67
.68
.69
.70
.71
.72
.73
.74
.75
.76
.77
.78
.79
.80
.81
.82
.83
.84
.85
.86
.87
.88
.89
.90
.91
.92
.93
.94
.95
.96
.97
.98
.99
.100
.101
.102
.103
.104
.105
.106
.107
.108
.109
.110
.111
.112
.113
.114
.115

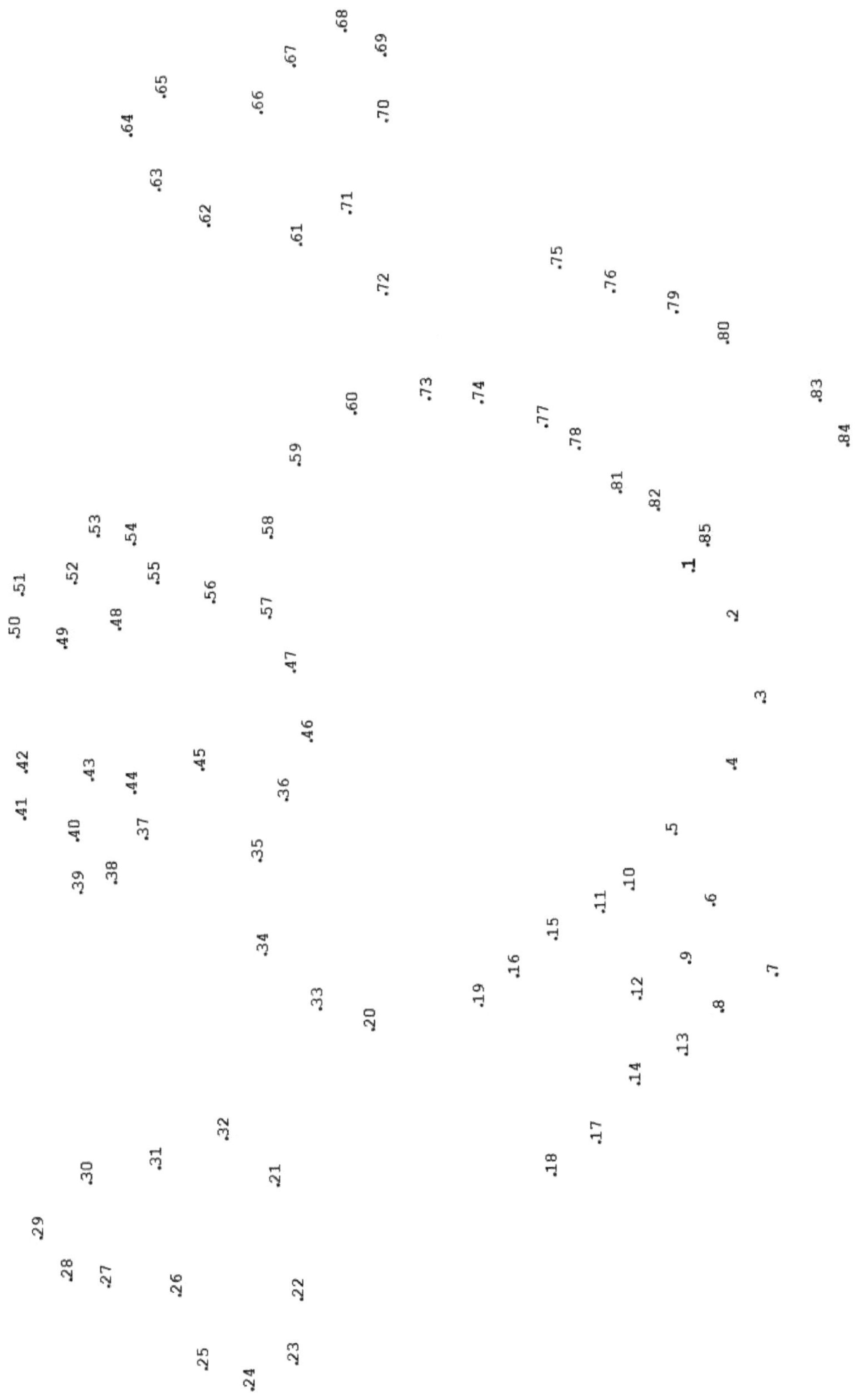

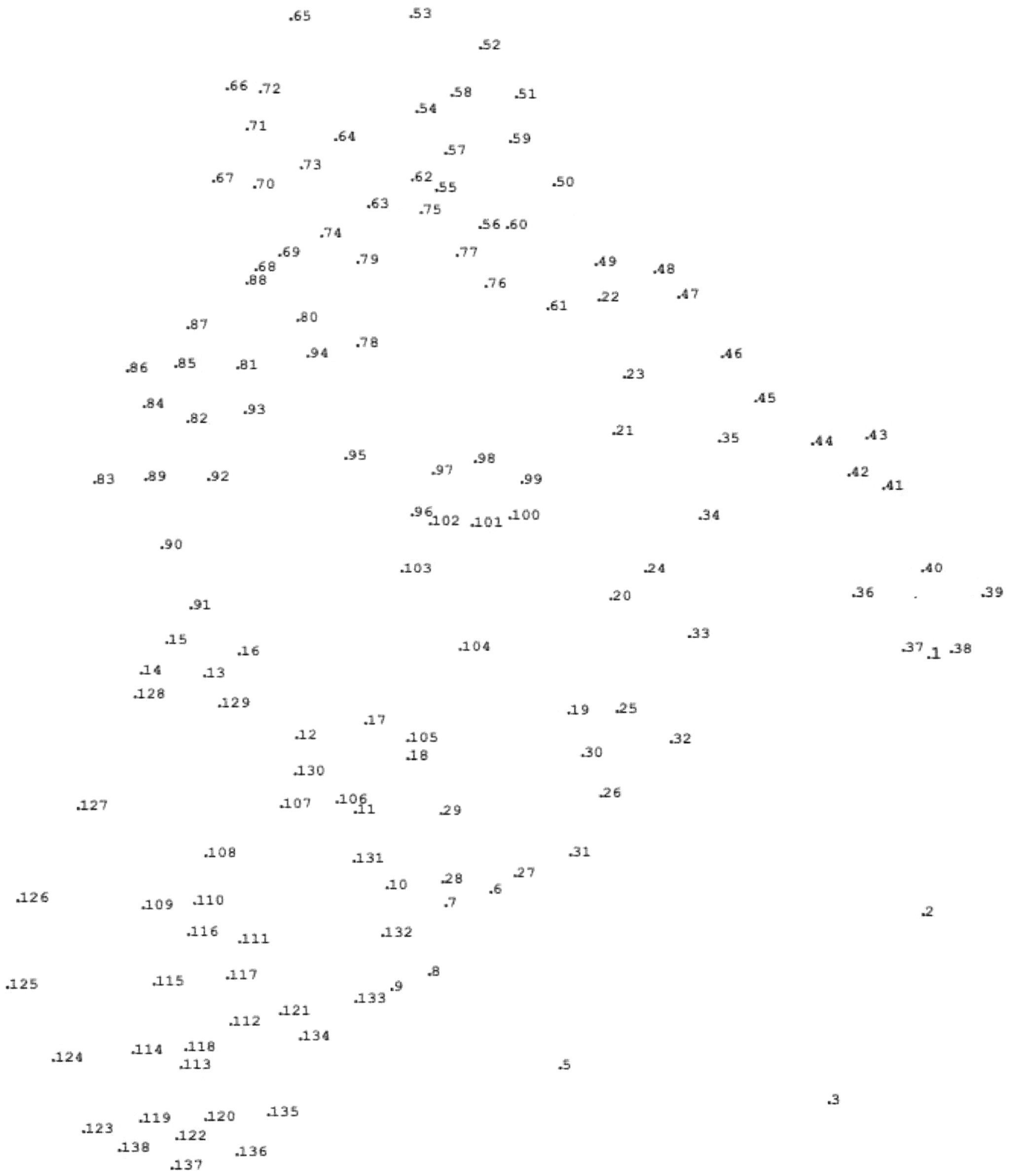
.65 .53
.52
.66 .72 .58 .51
.54
.71 .64 .59
.57
.73
.67 .70 .62 .55 .50
.63 .75
.56 .60
.74
.69 .79 .77 .49 .48
.68
.88 .76
.61 .22 .47
.87 .80
.78
.86 .85 .81 .94 .46
.23
.45
.84 .82 .93
.21 .35 .44 .43
.95 .98
.83 .89 .92 .97 .99 .42 .41
.96 .102 .101 .100 .34
.90
.103 .24 .40
.20 .36 .39
.91
.15 .16 .104 .33
.37 .1 .38
.14 .13
.128 .129
.19 .25
.17
.12 .105 .32
.18 .30
.130
.26
.127 .107 .106 .11 .29
.108 .131 .31
.28 .27
.126 .109 .110 .10 .6 .2
.7
.116 .111 .132
.8
.125 .115 .117 .9
.133
.121
.112
.134
.124 .114 .118
.113 .5
.3
.135
.123 .119 .120
.122
.138 .136
.137

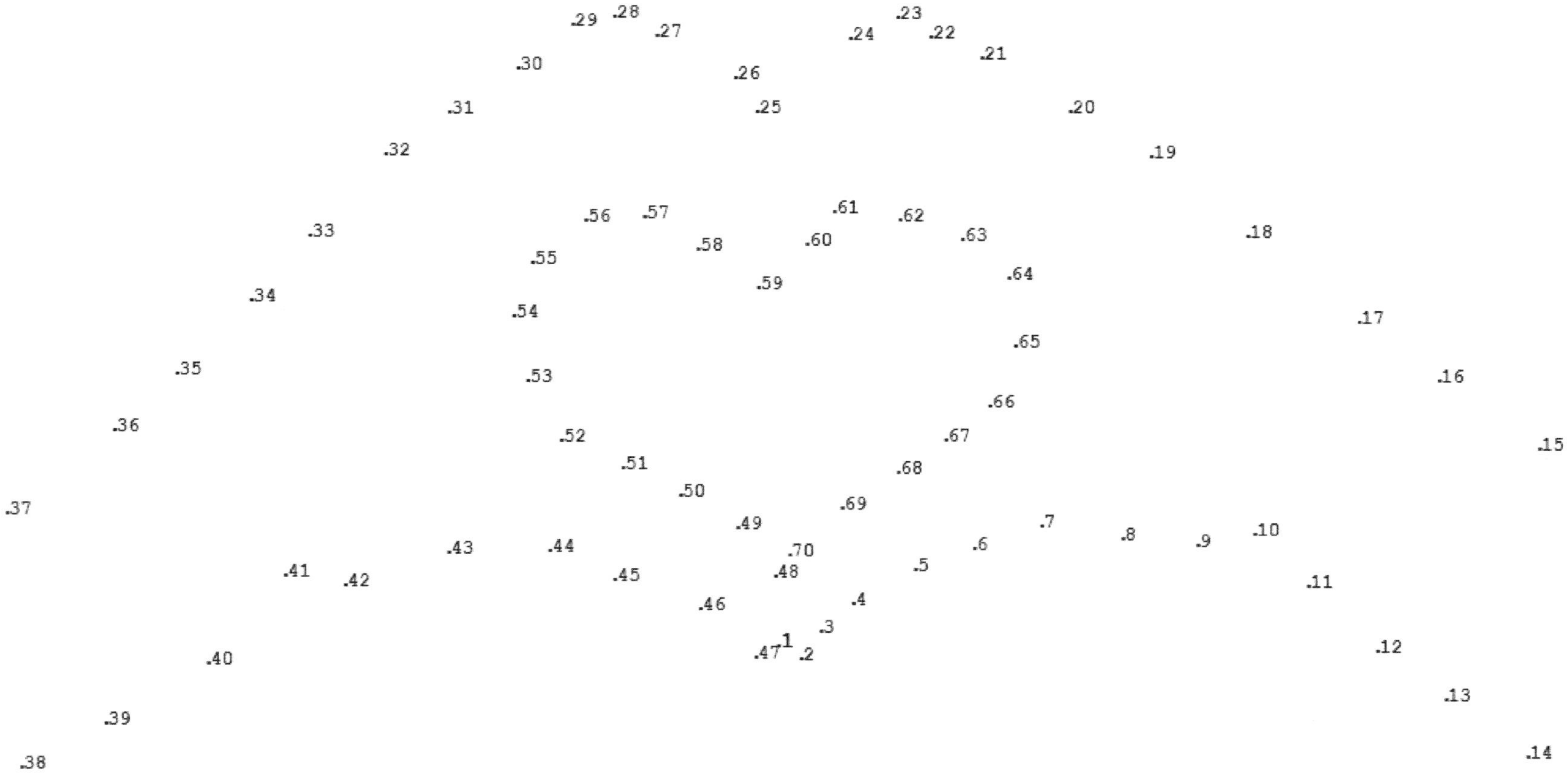
1
2
3
4
5
6
7
8
9
10
11
12
13
14
15
16
17
18
19
20
21
22
23
24
25
26
27
28
29
30
31
32
33
34
35
36
37
38
39
40
41
42
43
44
45
46
47
48
49
50
51
52
53
54
55
56
57
58
59
60
61
62
63
64
65
66
67
68
69
70

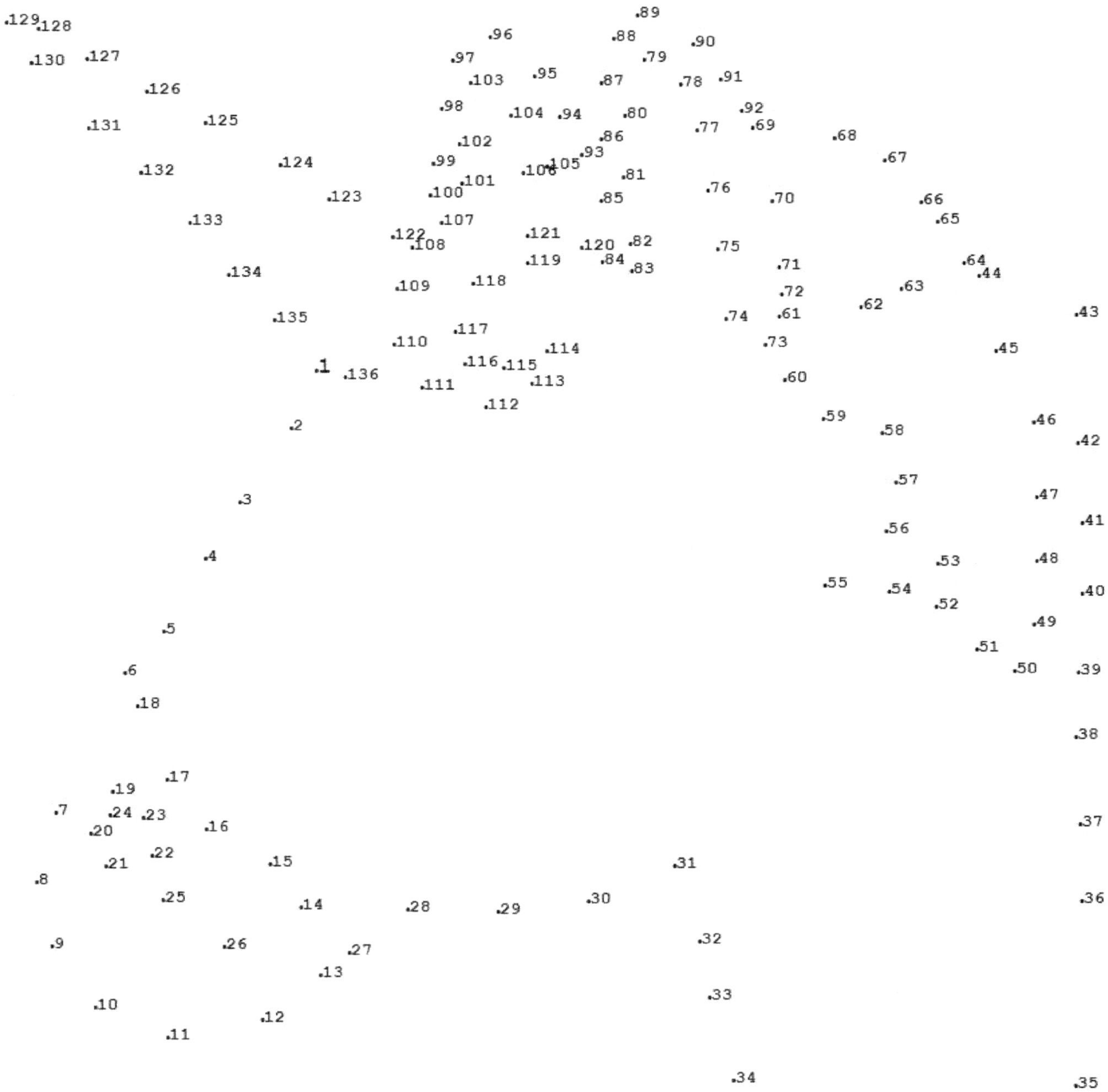
1
2
3
4
5
6
7
8
9
10
11
12
13
14
15
16
17
18
19
20
21
22
23
24
25
26
27
28
29
30
31
32
33
34
35
36
37
38
39
40
41
42
43
44
45
46
47
48
49
50
51
52
53
54
55
56
57
58
59
60
61
62
63
64
65
66
67
68
69
70
71
72
73
74
75
76
77
78
79
80
81
82
83
84
85
86
87
88
89
90
91
92
93
94
95
96
97
98
99
100
101
102
103
104
105
106
107
108
109
110
111
112
113
114
115
116
117
118
119
120
121
122
123
124
125
126
127
128
129
130
131
132
133
134
135
136

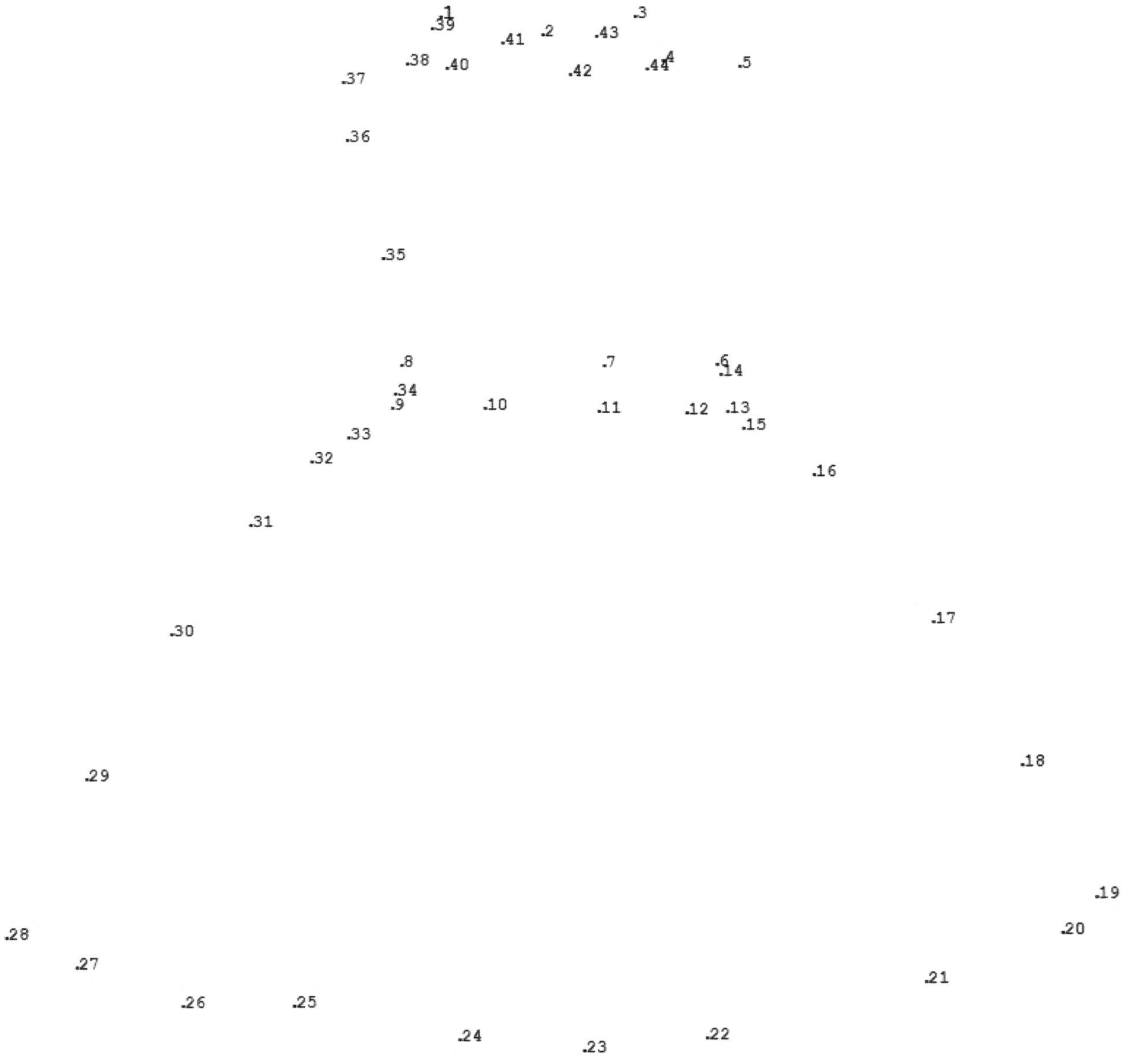
1
2
3
4
5
6
7
8
9
10
11
12
13
14
15
16
17
18
19
20
21
22
23
24
25
26
27
28
29
30
31
32
33
34
35
36
37
38
39
40
41
42
43
44

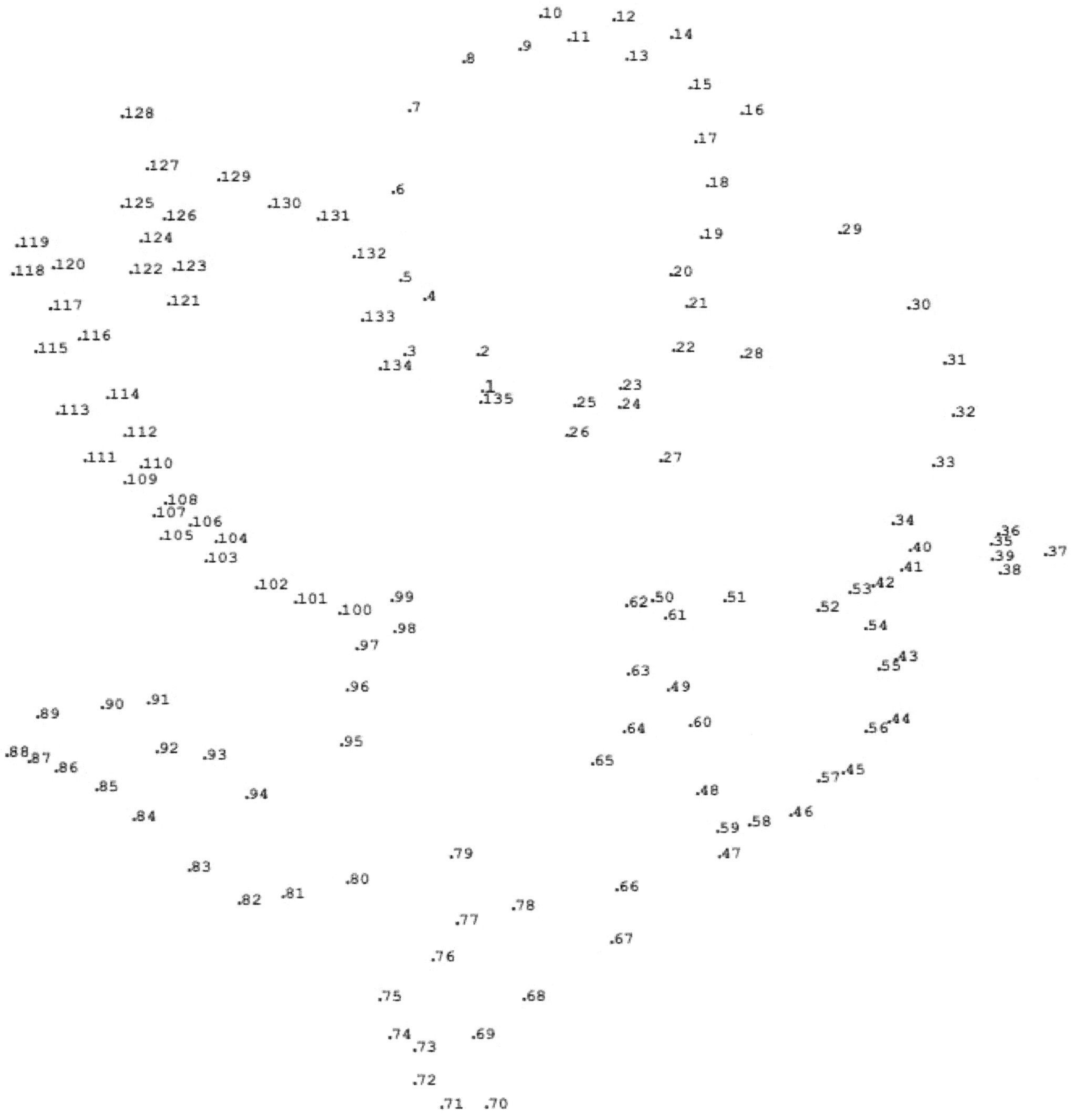

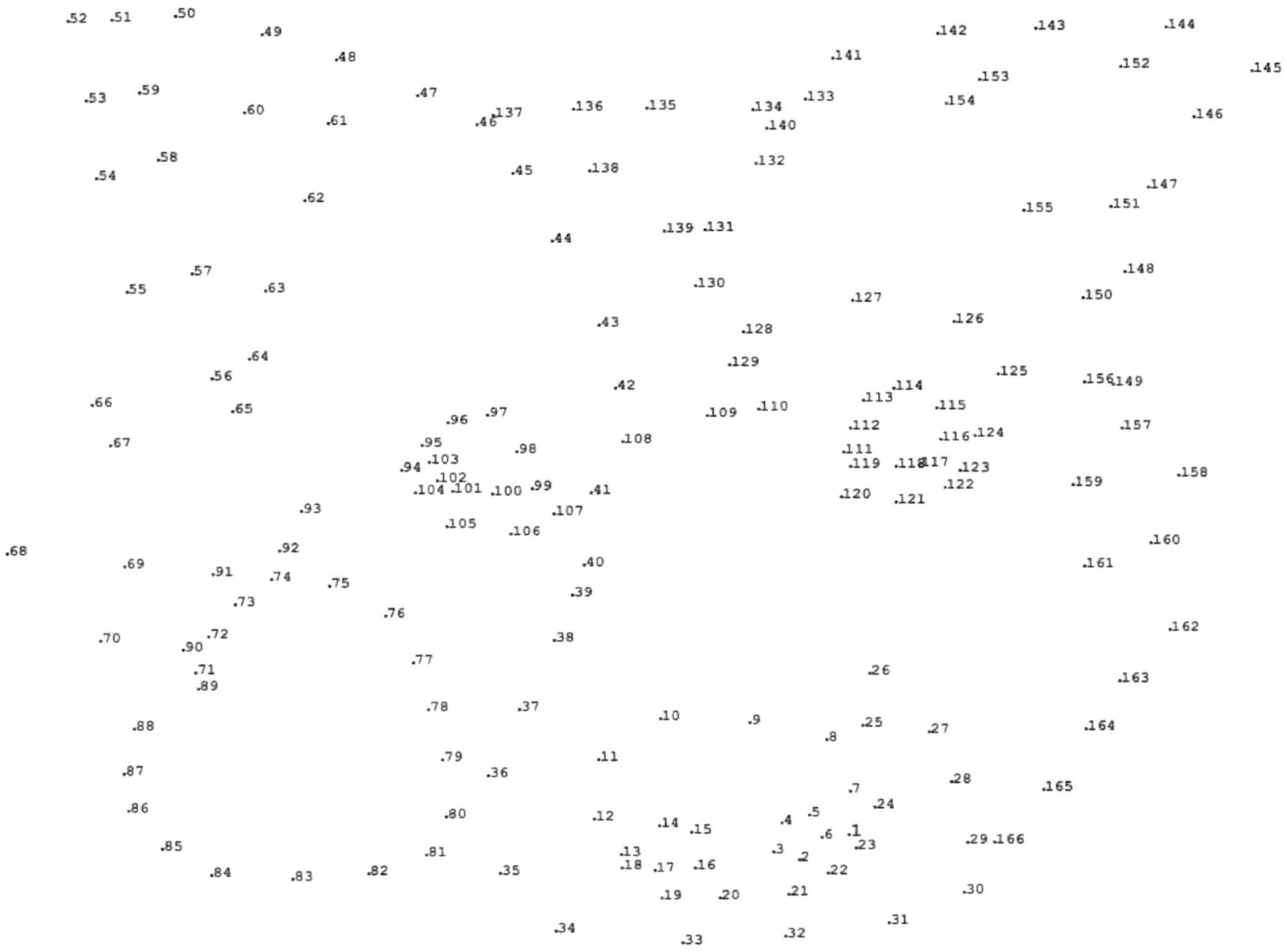

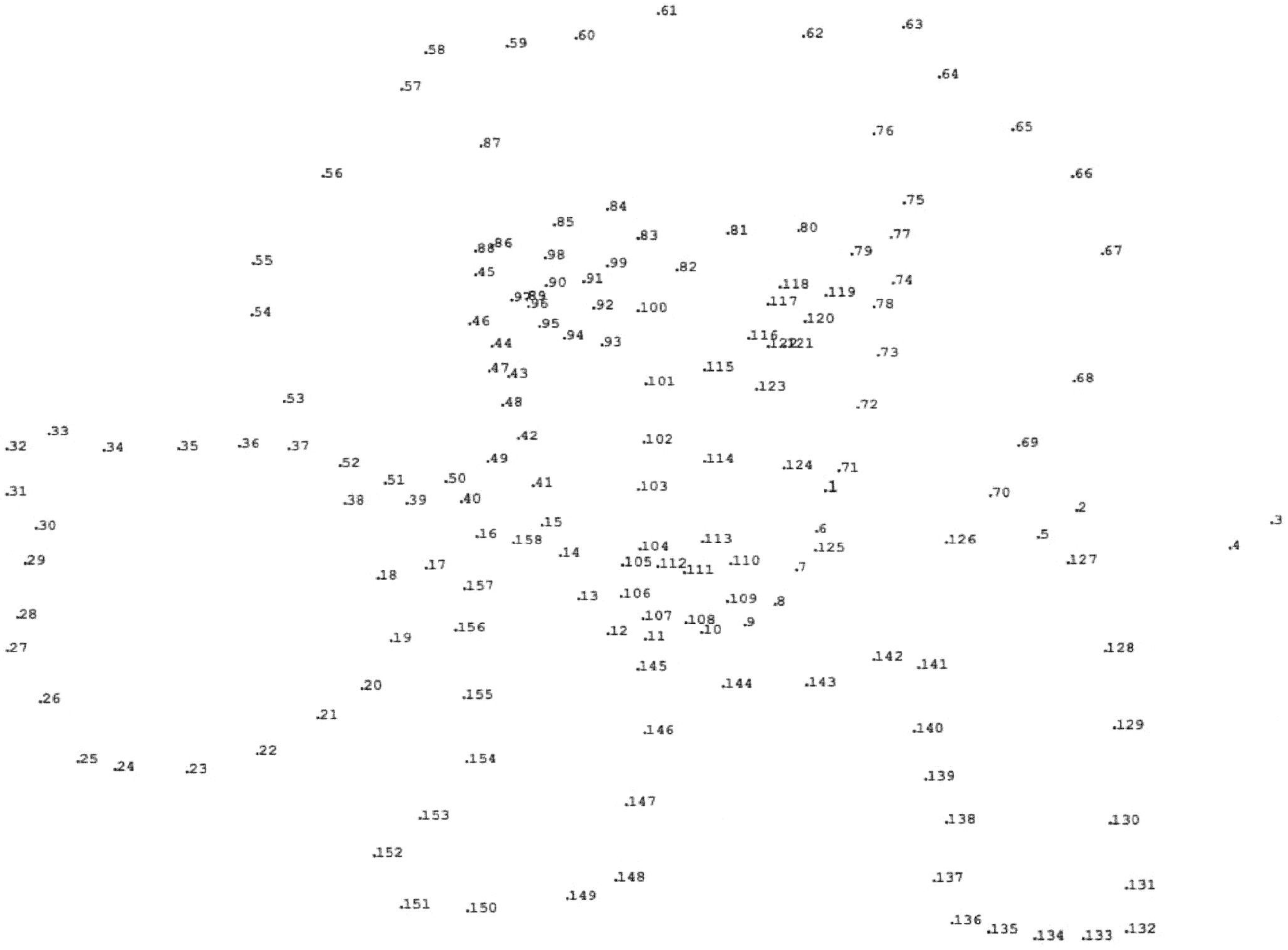

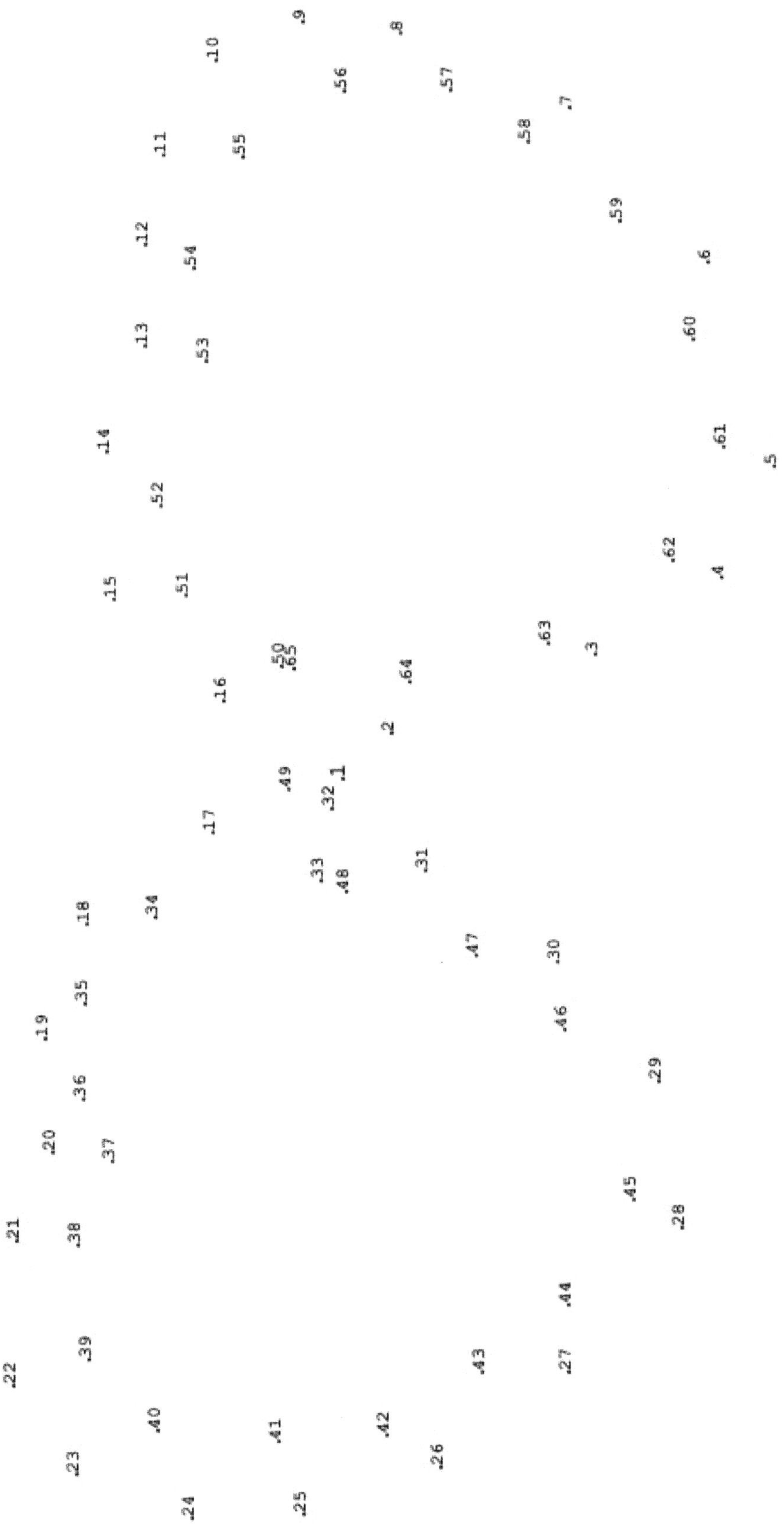

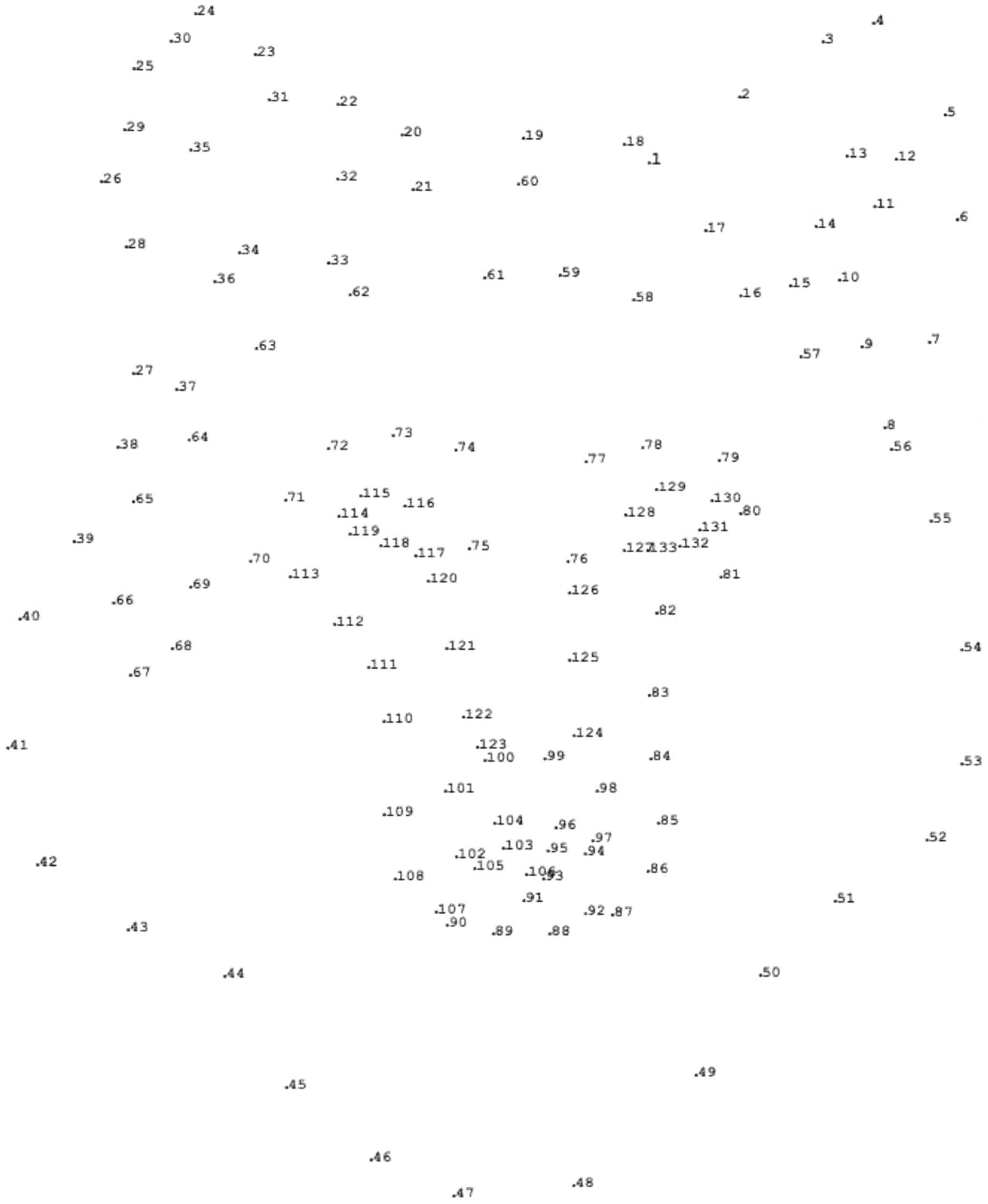
1 2 3 4 5 6 7 8 9 10 11 12 13 14 15 16 17 18 19 20 21 22 23 24 25 26 27 28 29 30 31 32 33 34 35 36 37 38 39 40 41 42 43 44 45 46 47 48 49 50 51 52 53 54 55 56 57 58 59 60 61 62 63 64 65 66 67 68 69 70 71 72 73 74 75 76 77 78 79 80 81 82 83 84 85 86 87 88 89 90 91 92 93 94 95 96 97 98 99 100 101 102 103 104 105 106 107 108 109 110 111 112 113 114 115 116 117 118 119 120 121 122 123 124 125 126 127 128 129 130 131 132 133

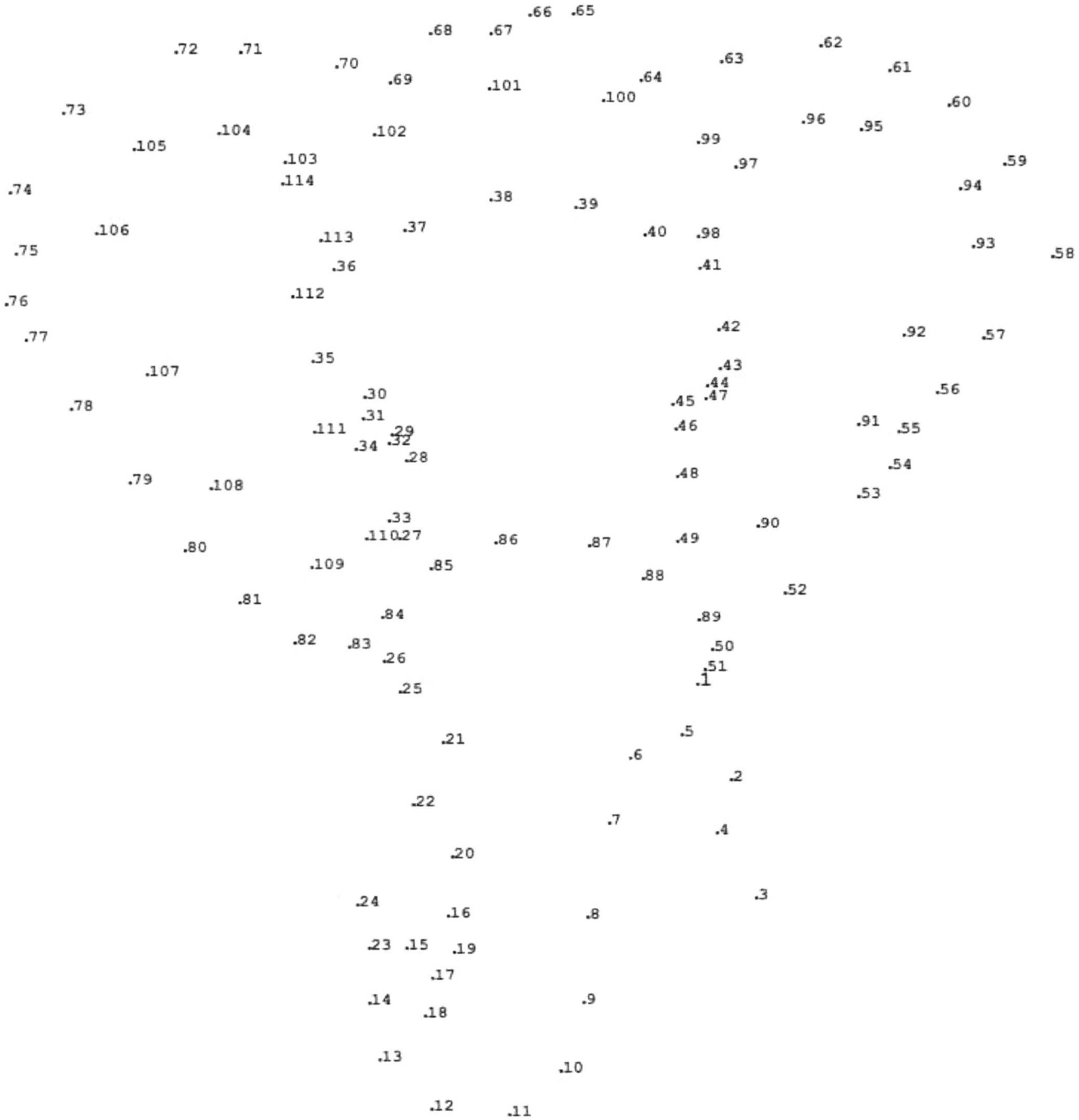

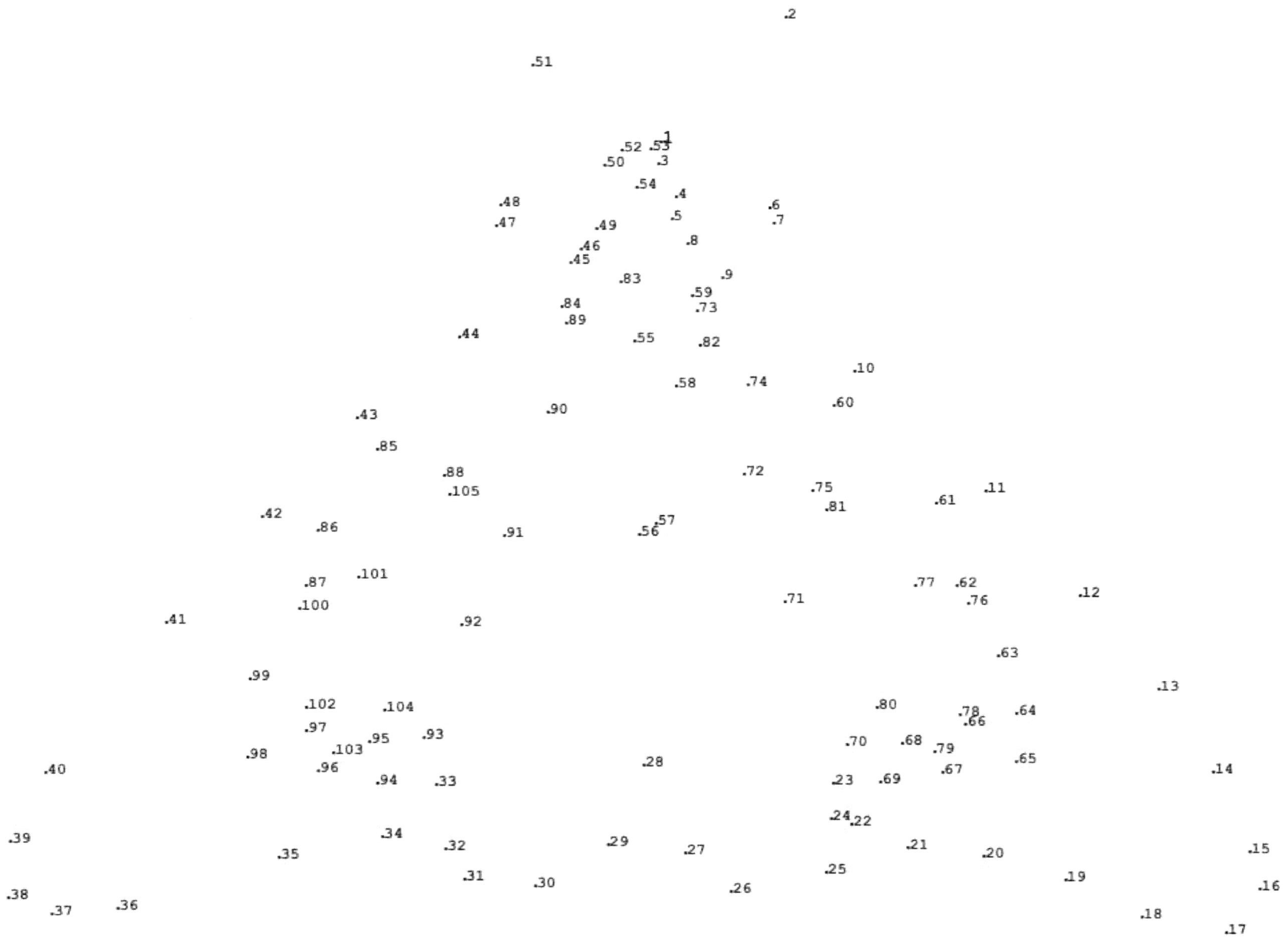

.1
.2
.3
.4
.5
.6
.7
.8
.9
.10
.11
.12
.13
.14
.15
.16
.17
.18
.19
.20
.21
.22
.23
.24
.25
.26
.27
.28
.29
.30
.31
.32
.33
.34
.35
.36
.37
.38
.39
.40
.41
.42
.43
.44
.45
.46
.47
.48
.49
.50
.51
.52
.53
.54
.55
.56
.57
.58
.59
.60
.61
.62
.63
.64
.65
.66
.67
.68
.69
.70
.71
.72
.73
.74
.75
.76
.77
.78
.79
.80
.81
.82
.83
.84
.85
.86
.87
.88
.89
.90
.91
.92
.93
.94
.95
.96
.97
.98
.99
.100
.101
.102
.103
.104
.105

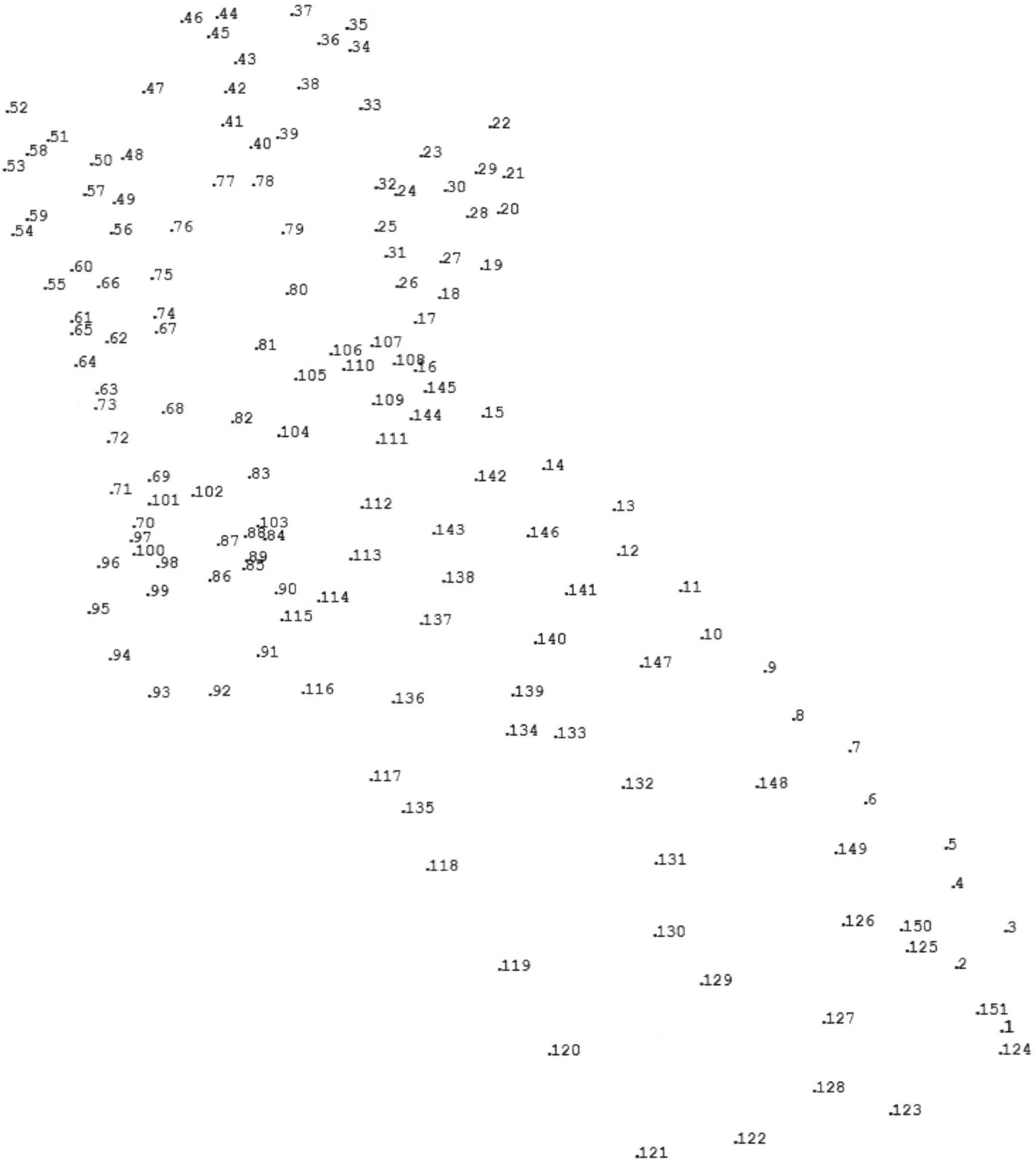

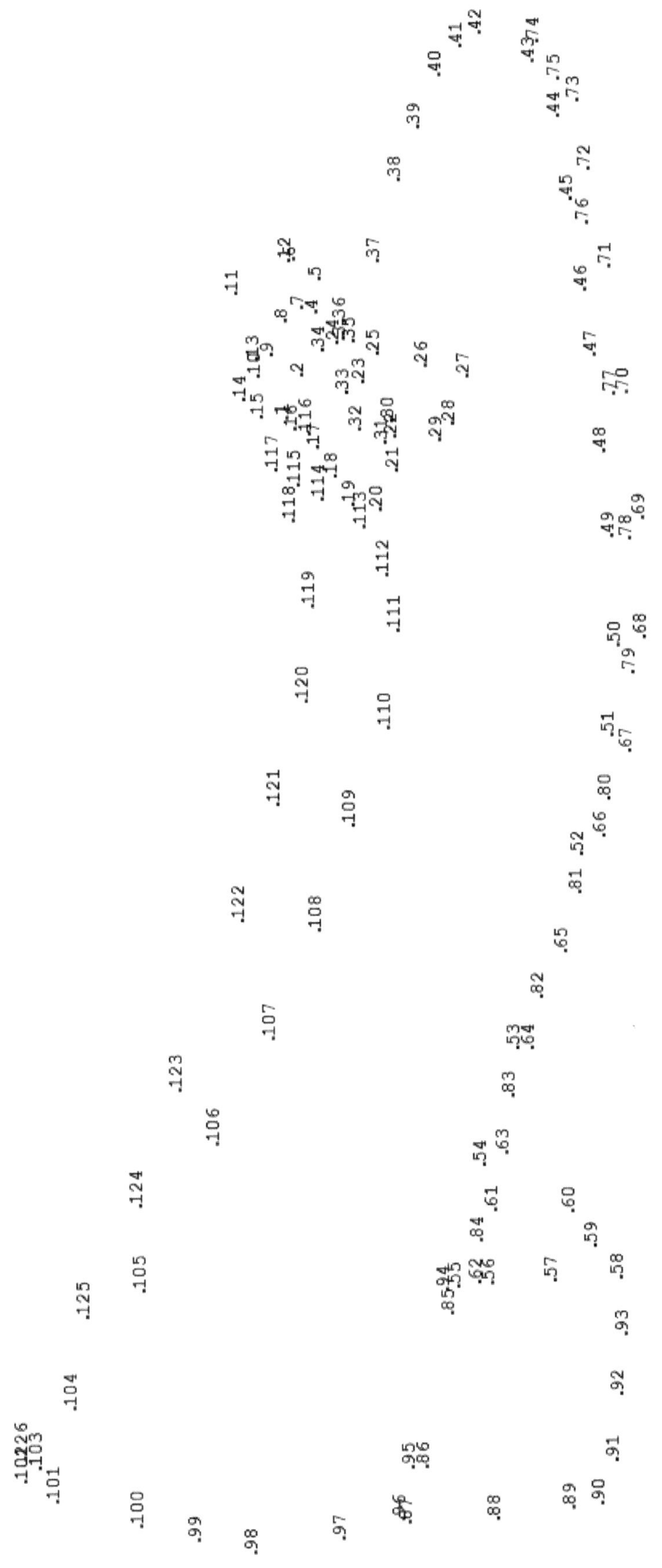

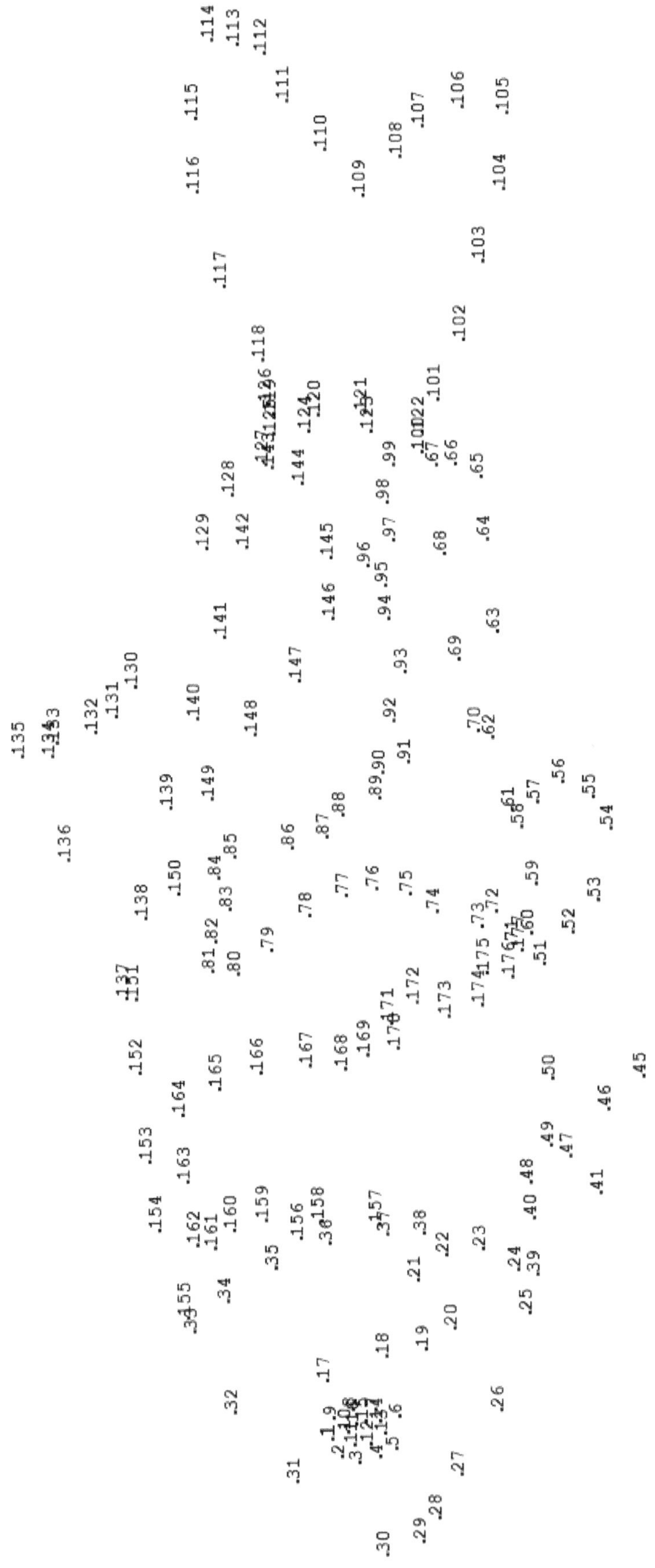

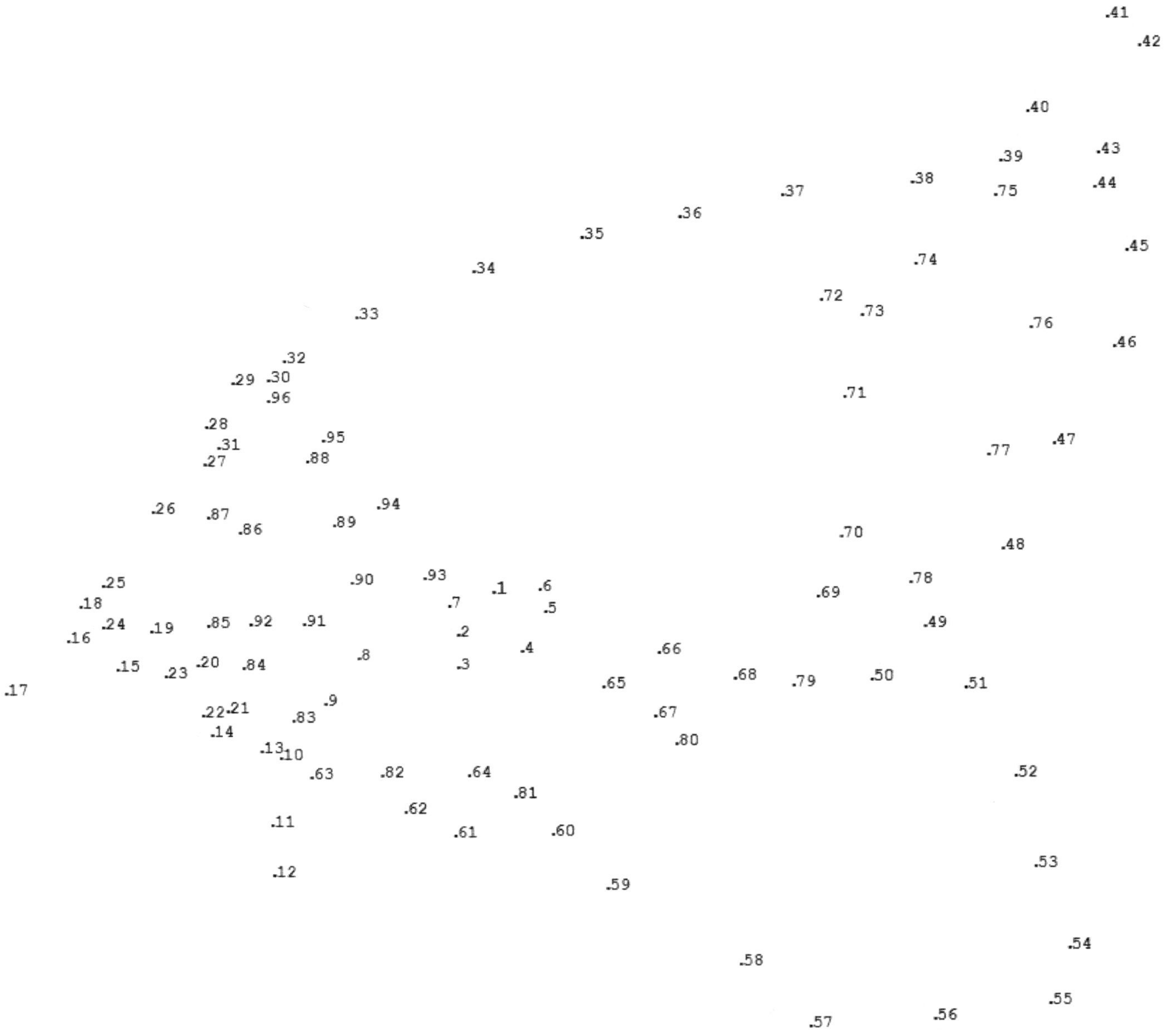

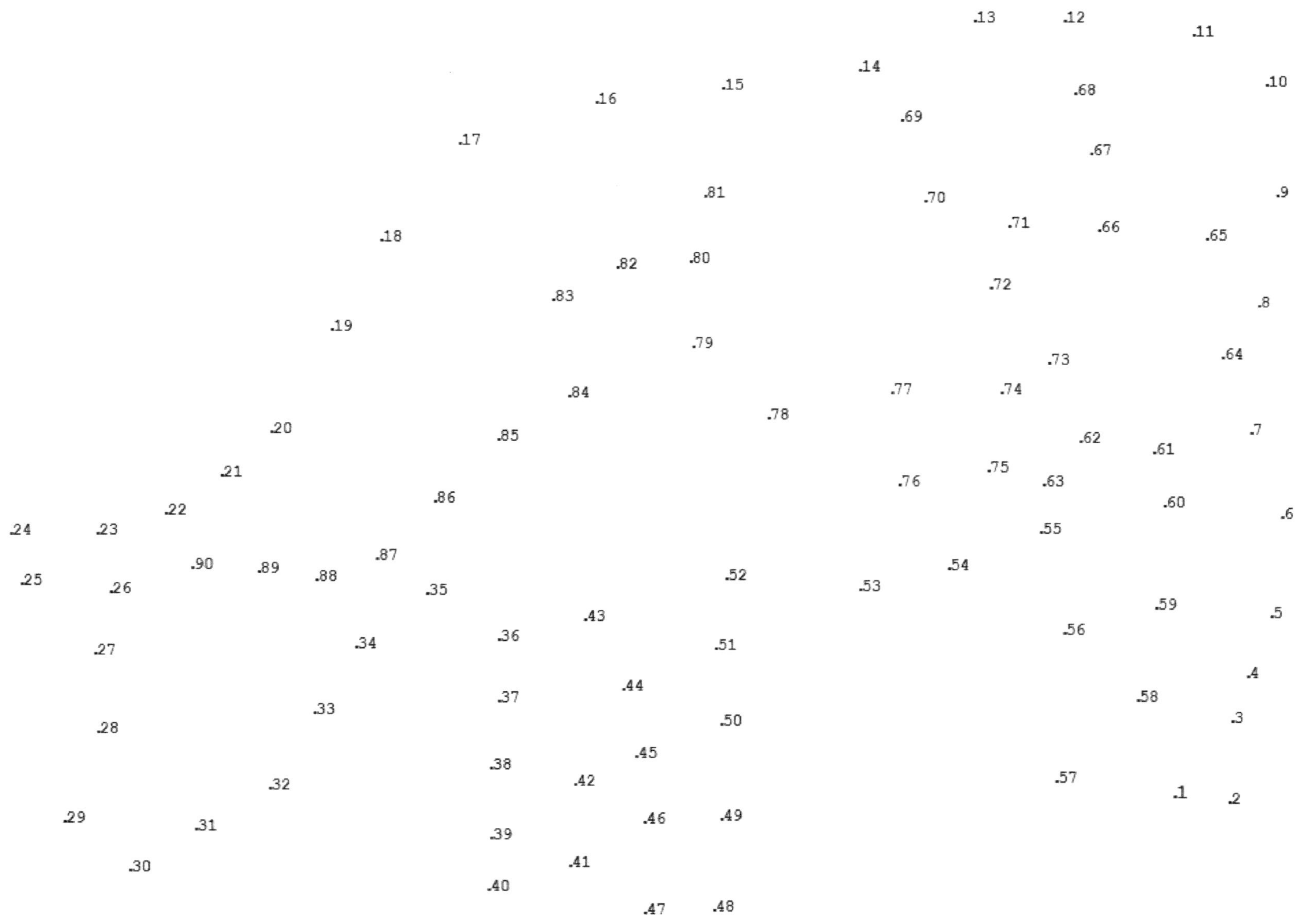

.1
.2
.3
.4
.5
.6
.7
.8
.9
.10
.11
.12
.13
.14
.15
.16
.17
.18
.19
.20
.21
.22
.23
.24
.25
.26
.27
.28
.29
.30
.31
.32
.33
.34
.35
.36
.37
.38
.39
.40
.41
.42
.43
.44
.45
.46
.47
.48
.49
.50
.51
.52
.53
.54
.55
.56
.57
.58
.59
.60
.61
.62
.63
.64
.65
.66
.67
.68
.69
.70
.71
.72
.73
.74
.75
.76
.77
.78
.79
.80
.81
.82
.83
.84
.85
.86
.87
.88
.89
.90

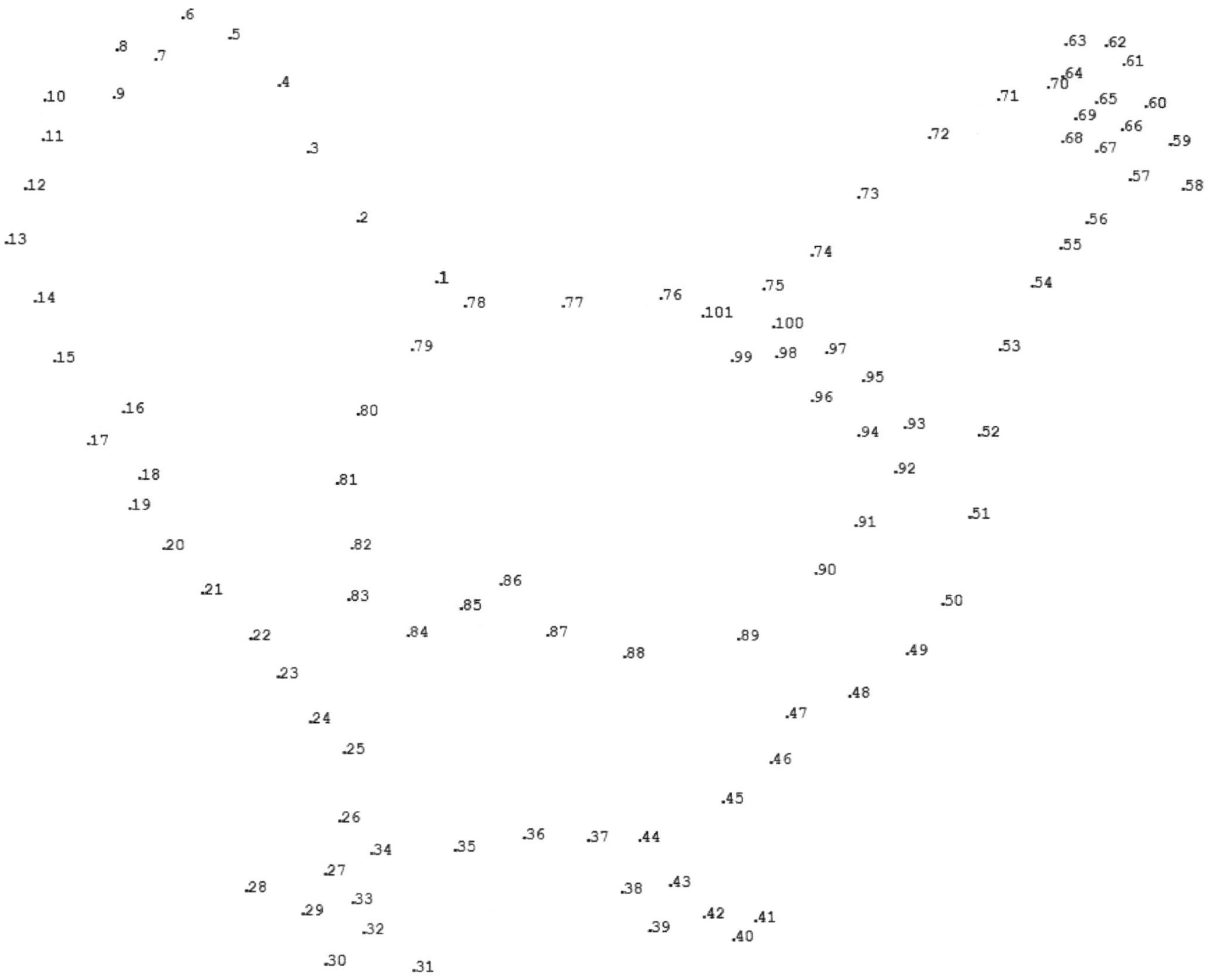

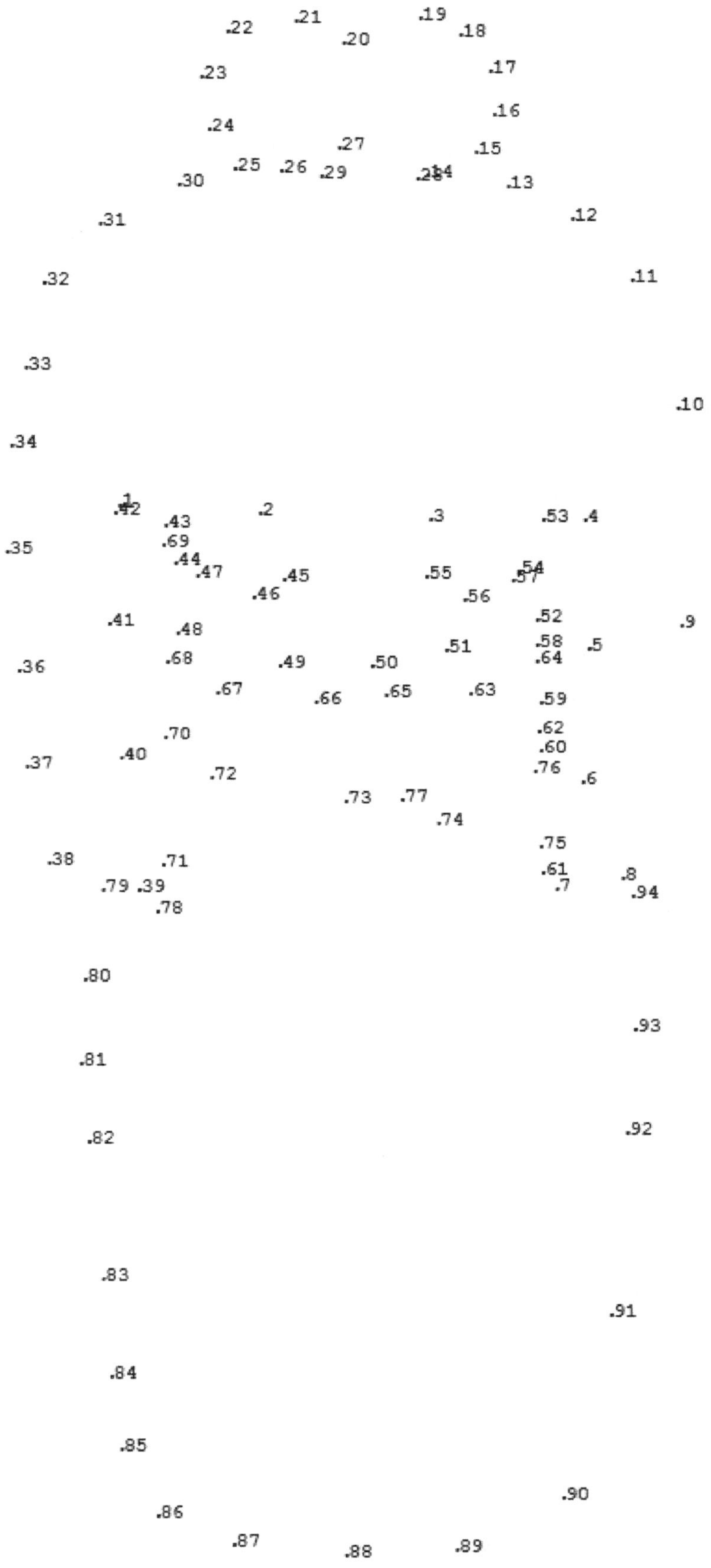
1
2
3
4
5
6
7
8
9
10
11
12
13
14
15
16
17
18
19
20
21
22
23
24
25
26
27
28
29
30
31
32
33
34
35
36
37
38
39
40
41
42
43
44
45
46
47
48
49
50
51
52
53
54
55
56
57
58
59
60
61
62
63
64
65
66
67
68
69
70
71
72
73
74
75
76
77
78
79
80
81
82
83
84
85
86
87
88
89
90
91
92
93
94

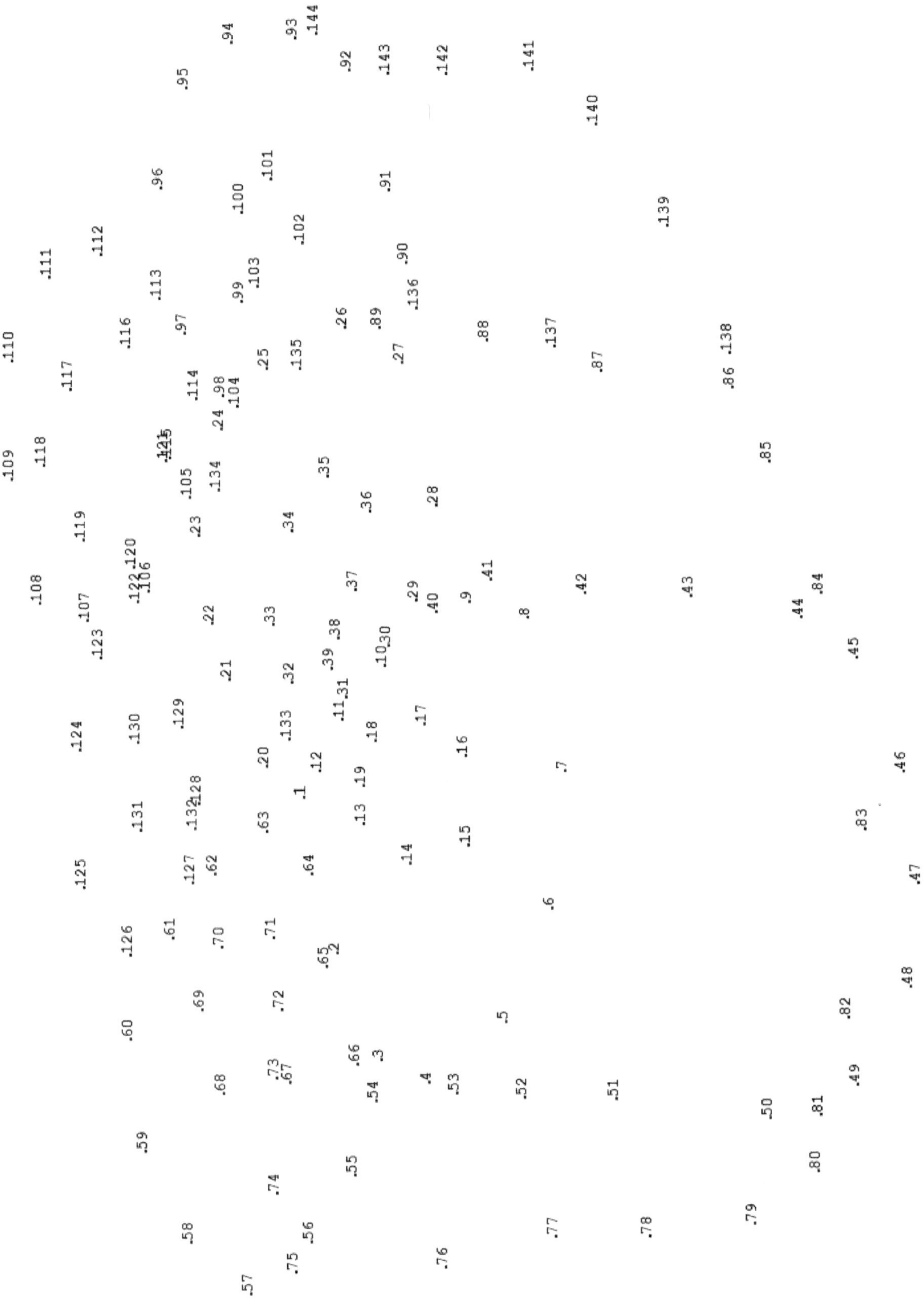

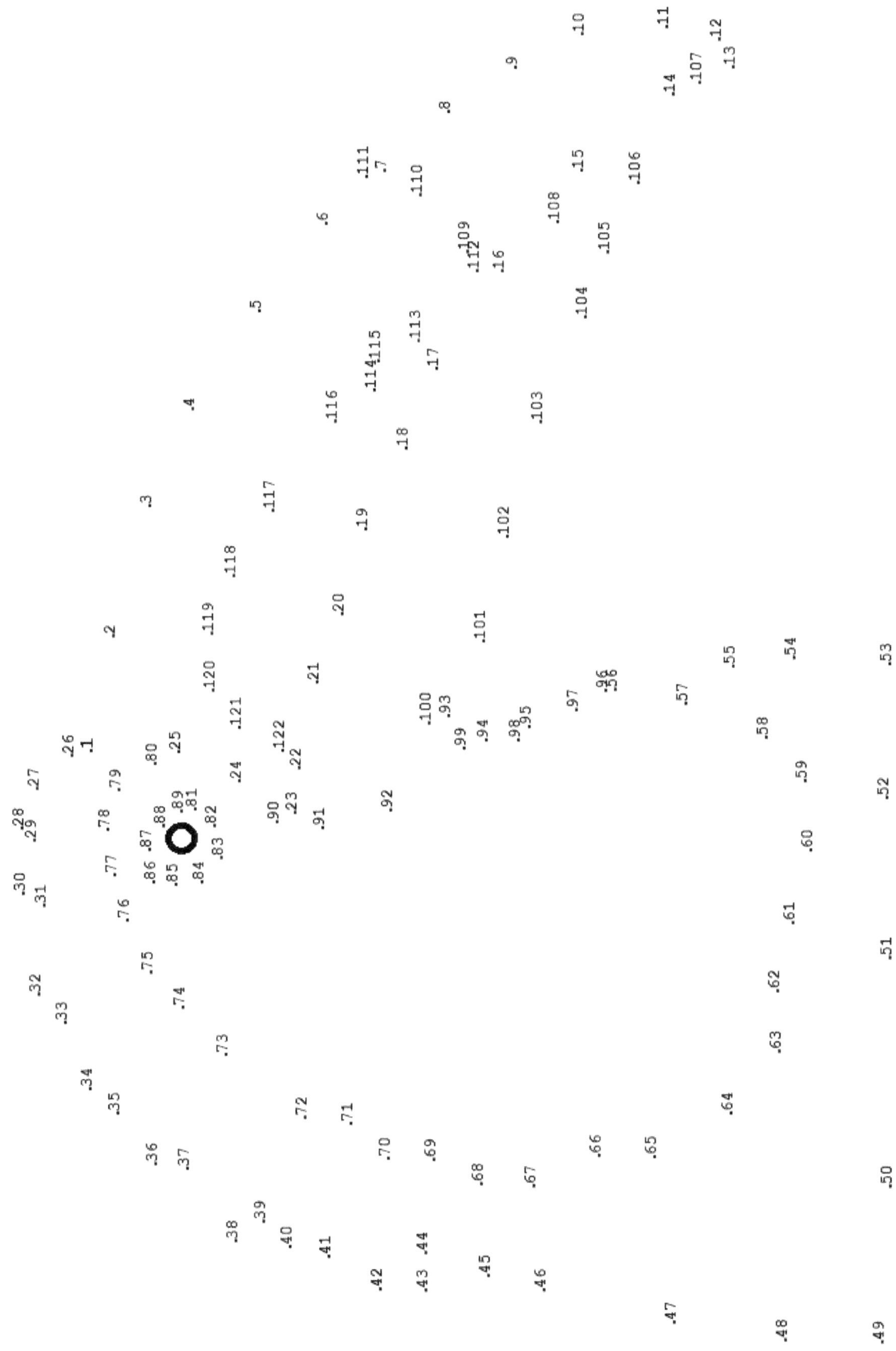

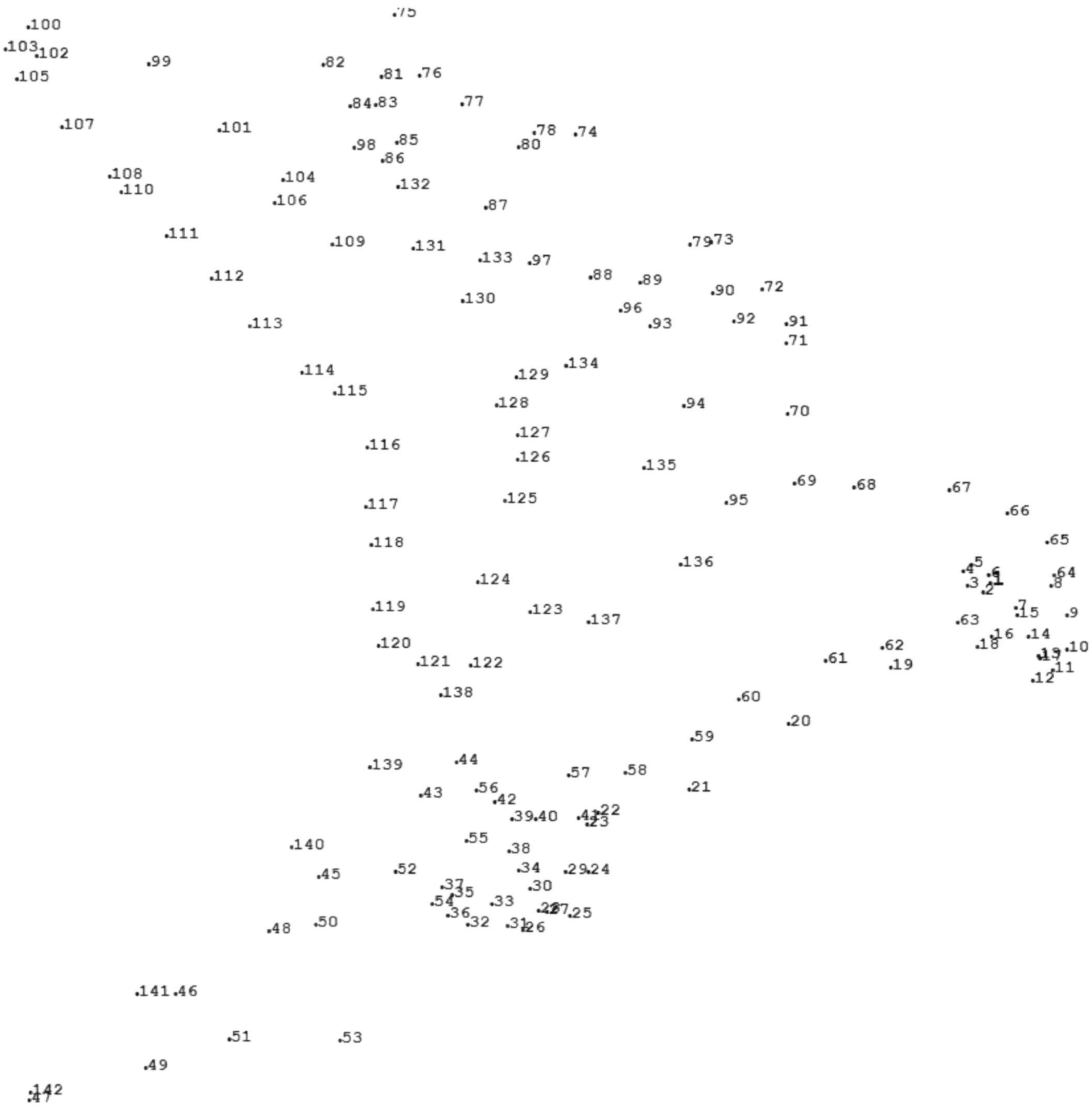

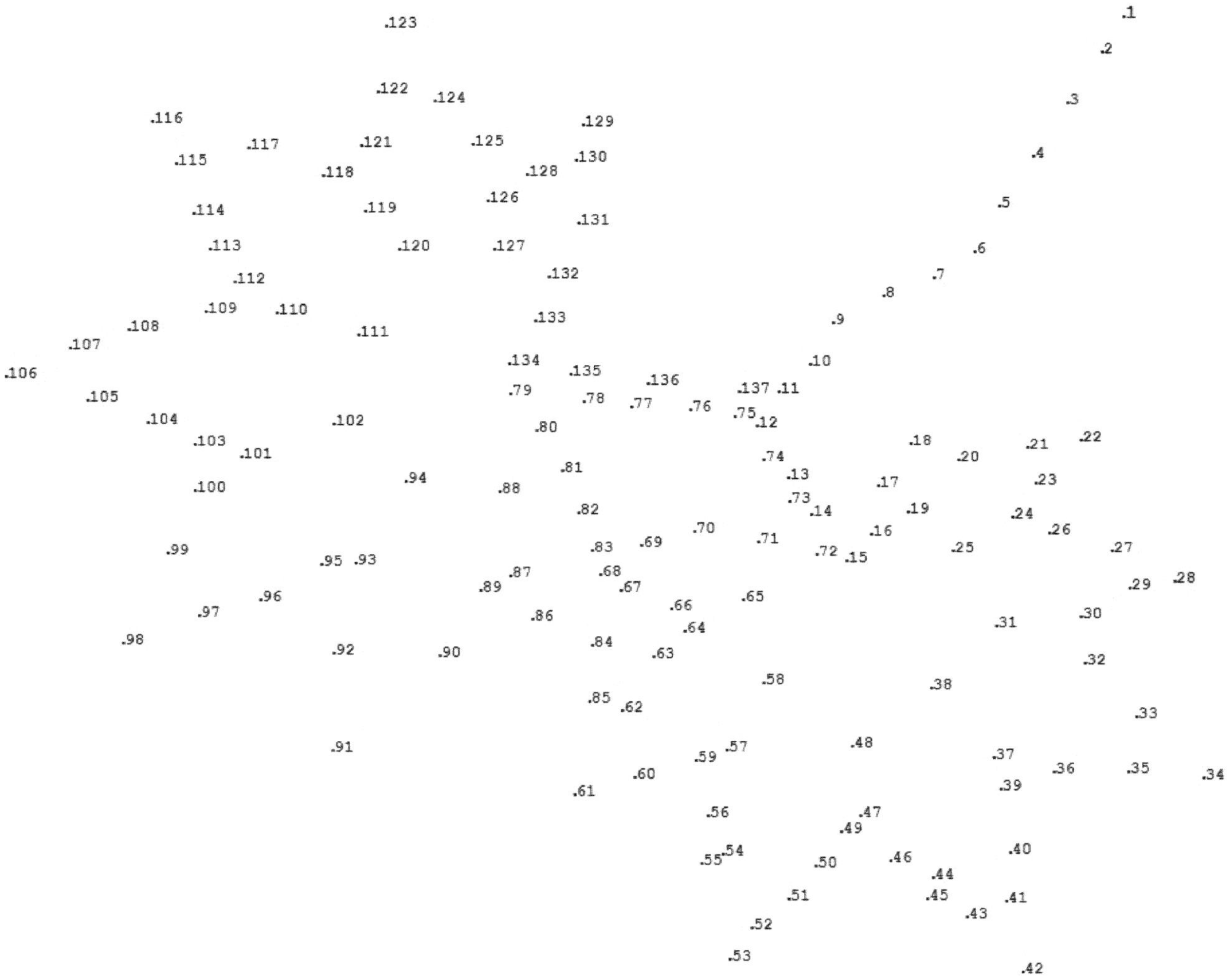

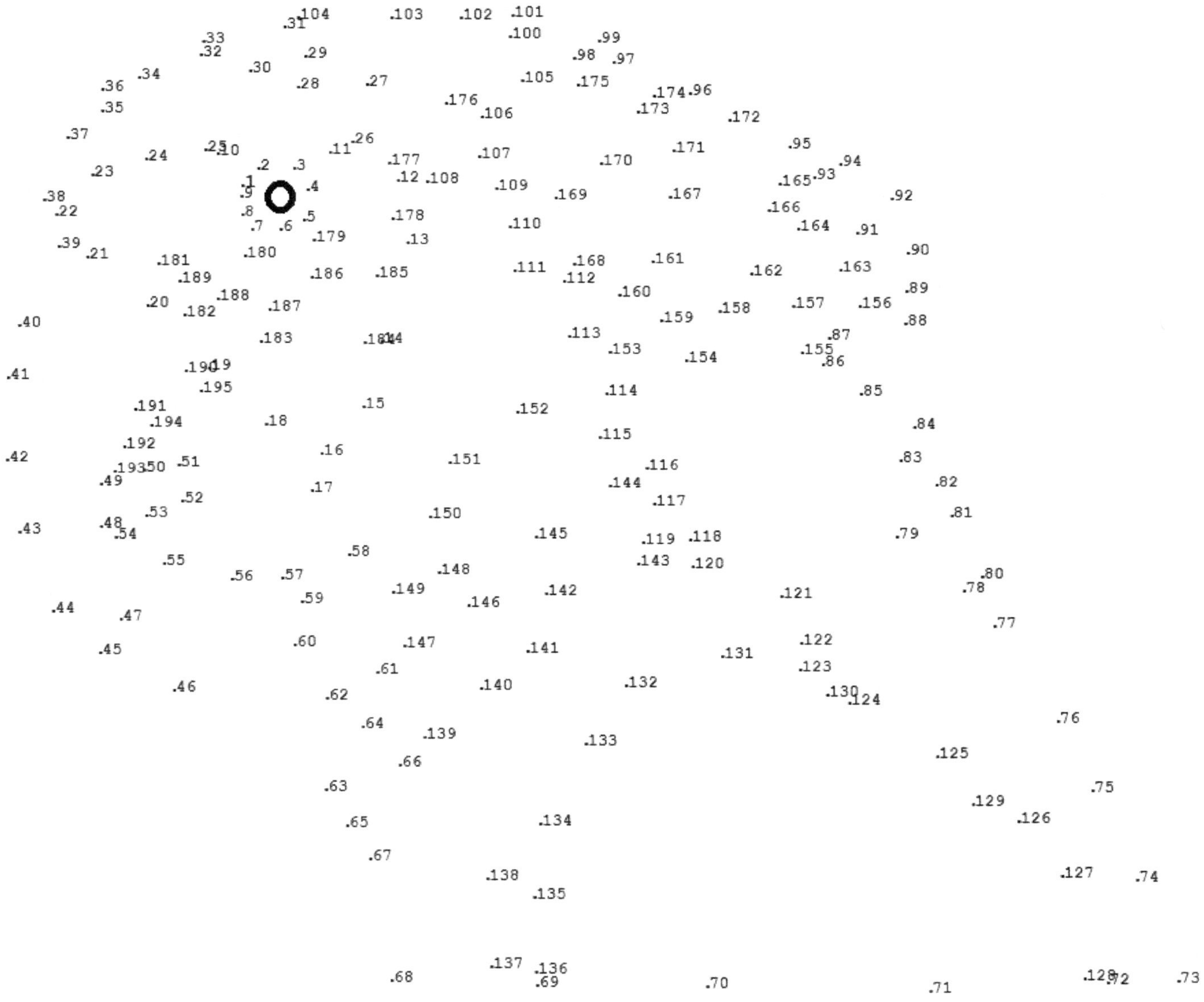

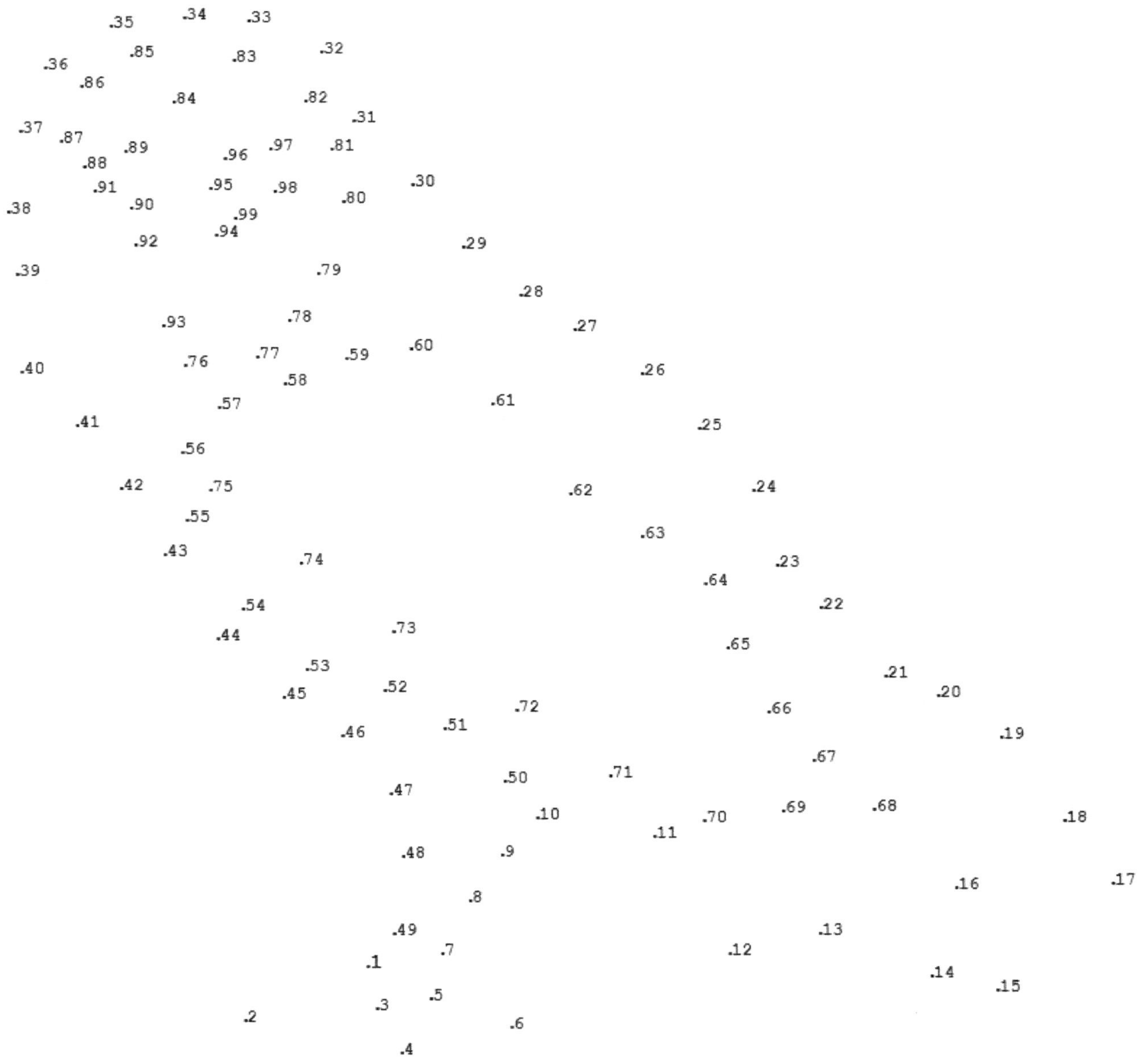

1
2
3
4
5
6
7
8
9
10
11
12
13
14
15
16
17
18
19
20
21
22
23
24
25
26
27
28
29
30
31
32
33
34
35
36
37
38
39
40
41
42
43
44
45
46
47
48
49
50
51
52
53
54
55
56
57
58
59
60
61
62
63
64
65
66
67
68
69
70
71
72
73
74
75
76
77
78
79
80
81
82
83
84
85
86
87
88
89
90
91
92
93
94
95
96
97
98
99

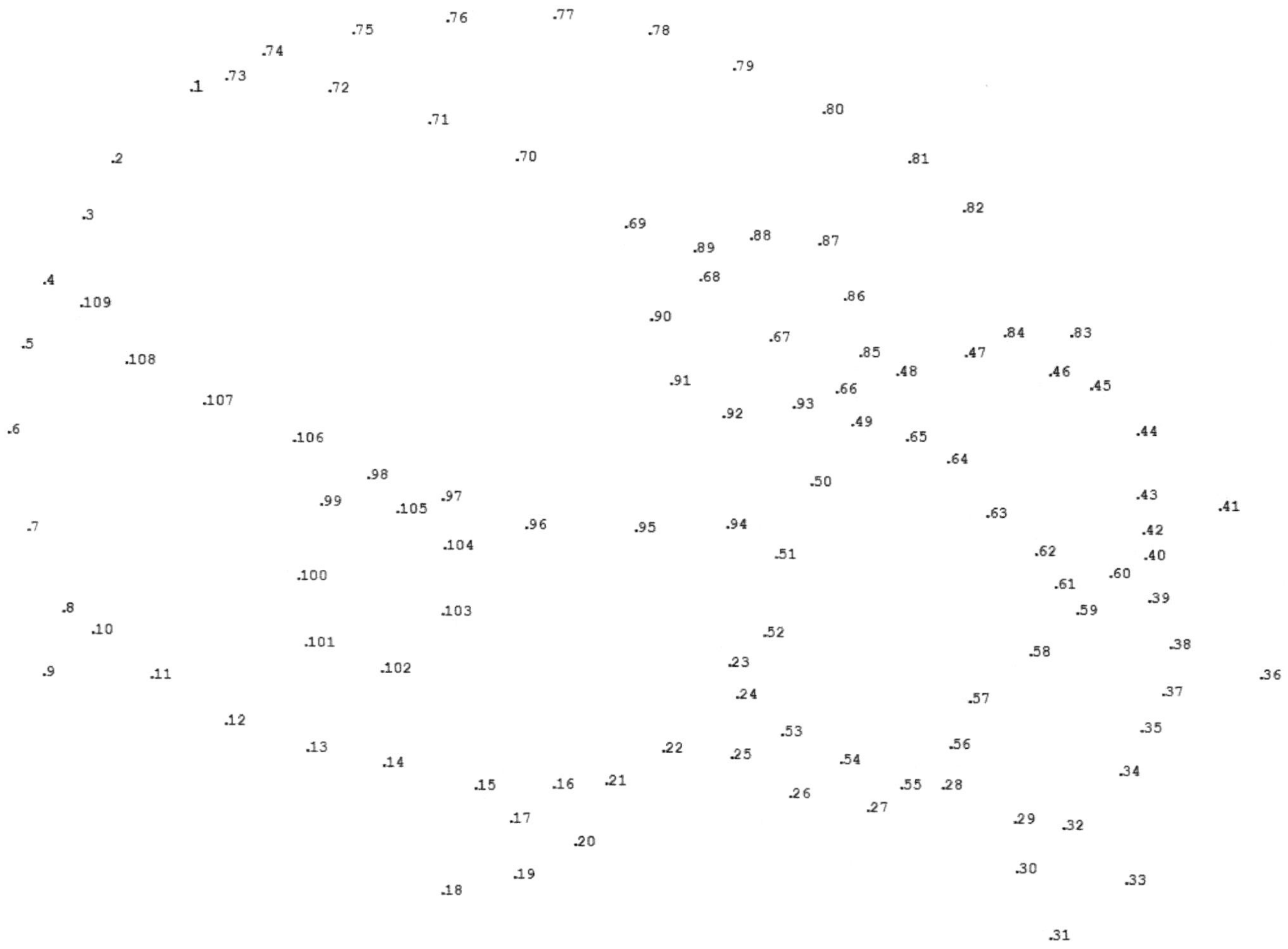
1
2
3
4
5
6
7
8
9
10
11
12
13
14
15
16
17
18
19
20
21
22
23
24
25
26
27
28
29
30
31
32
33
34
35
36
37
38
39
40
41
42
43
44
45
46
47
48
49
50
51
52
53
54
55
56
57
58
59
60
61
62
63
64
65
66
67
68
69
70
71
72
73
74
75
76
77
78
79
80
81
82
83
84
85
86
87
88
89
90
91
92
93
94
95
96
97
98
99
100
101
102
103
104
105
106
107
108
109

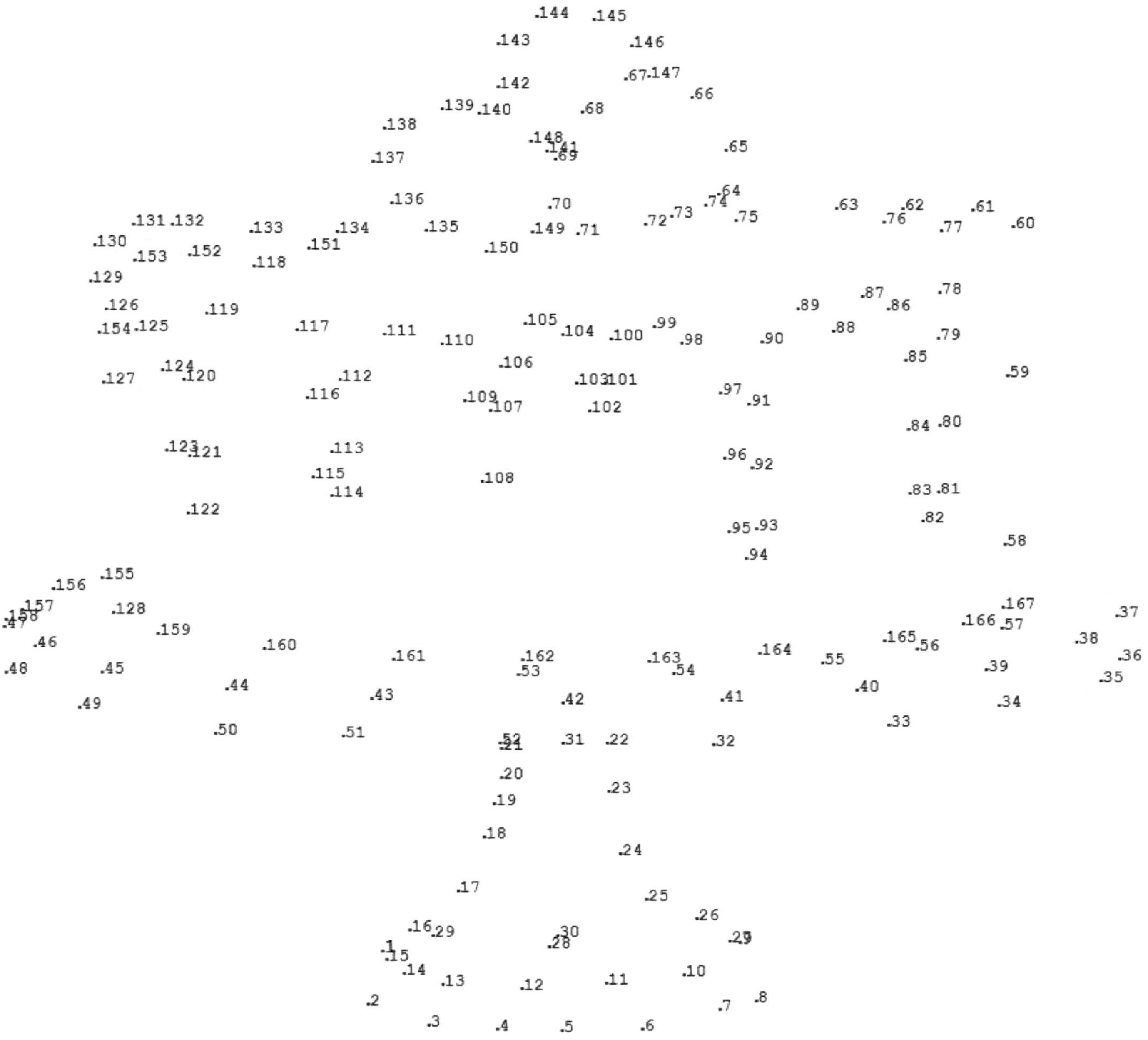

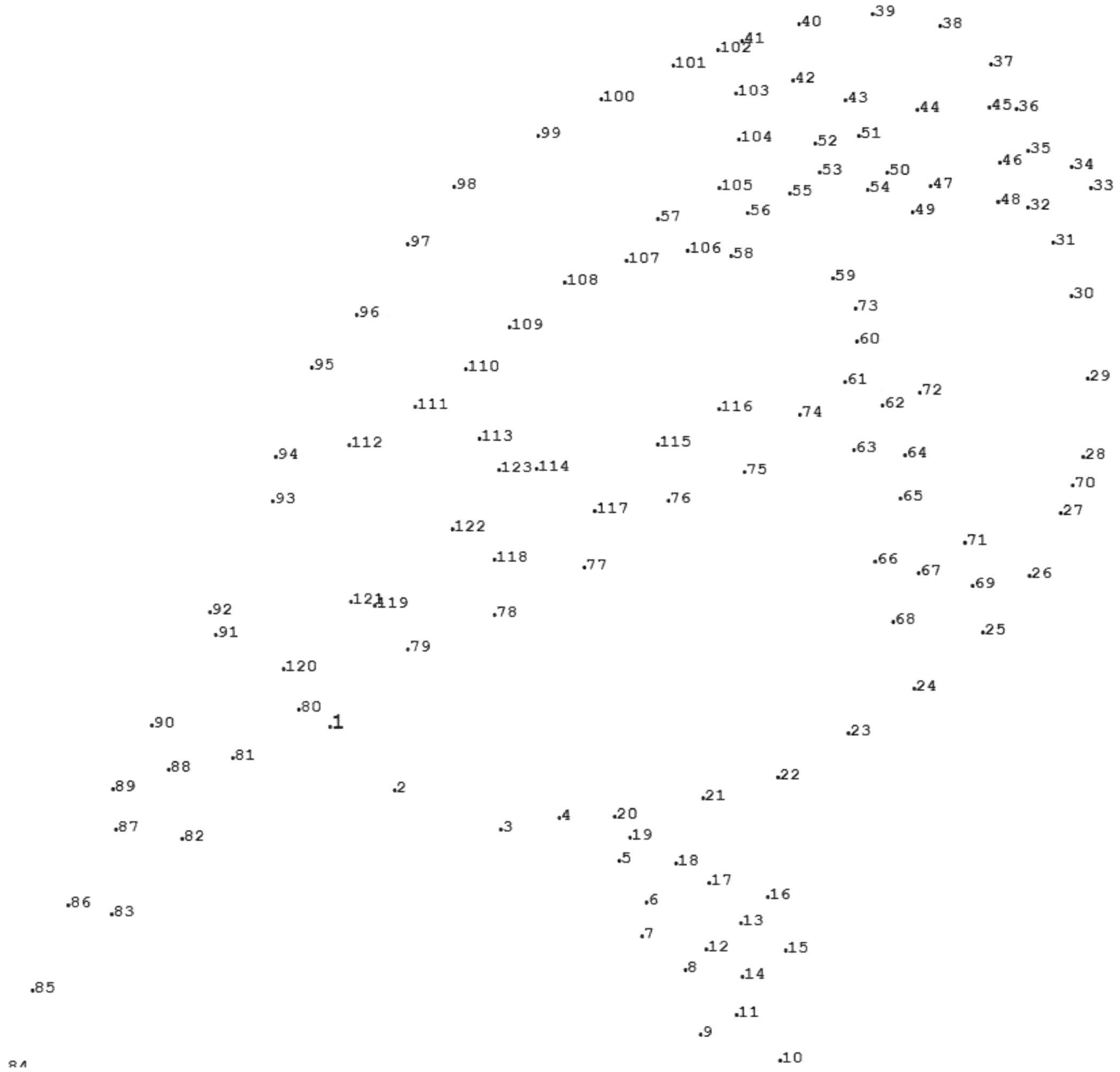

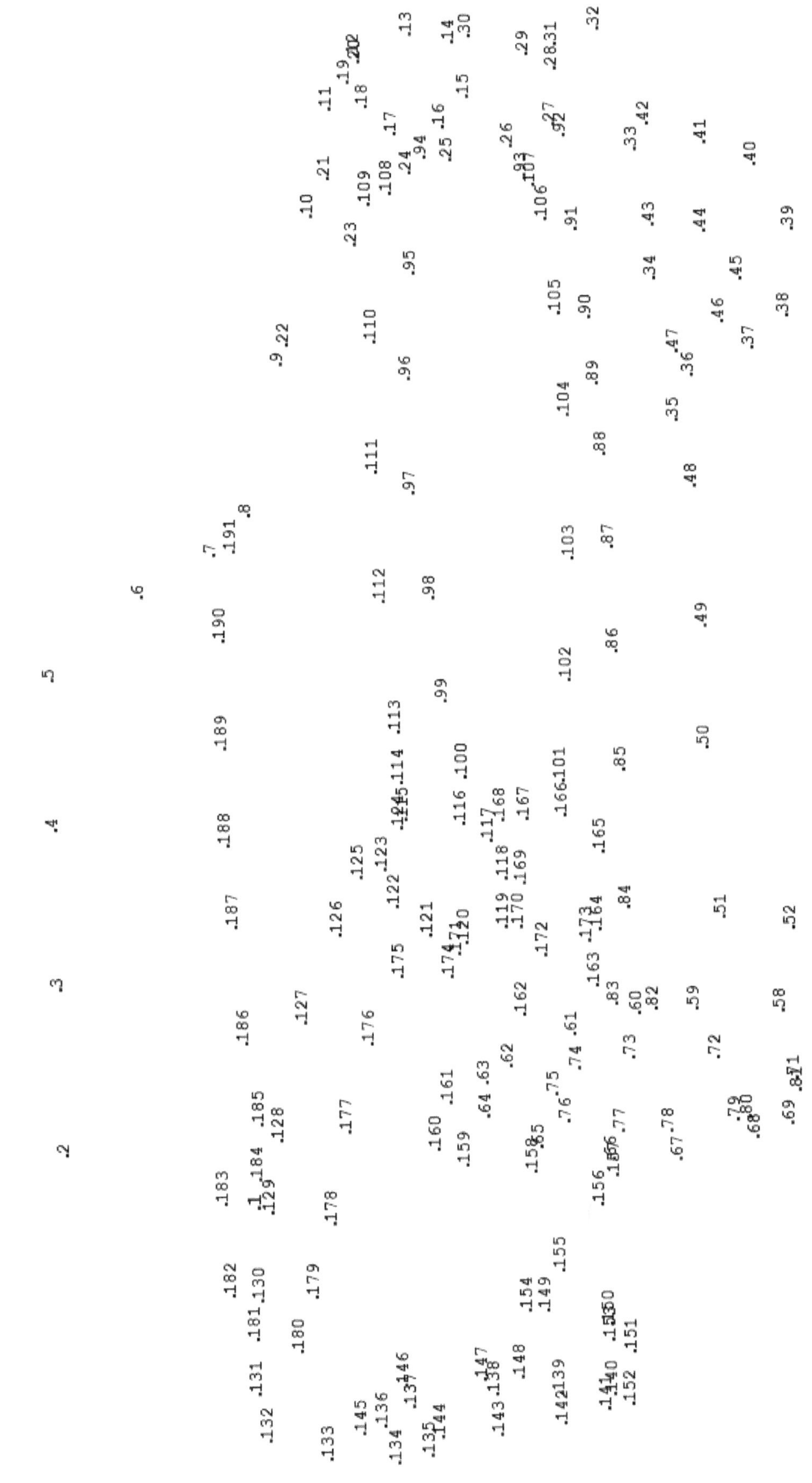

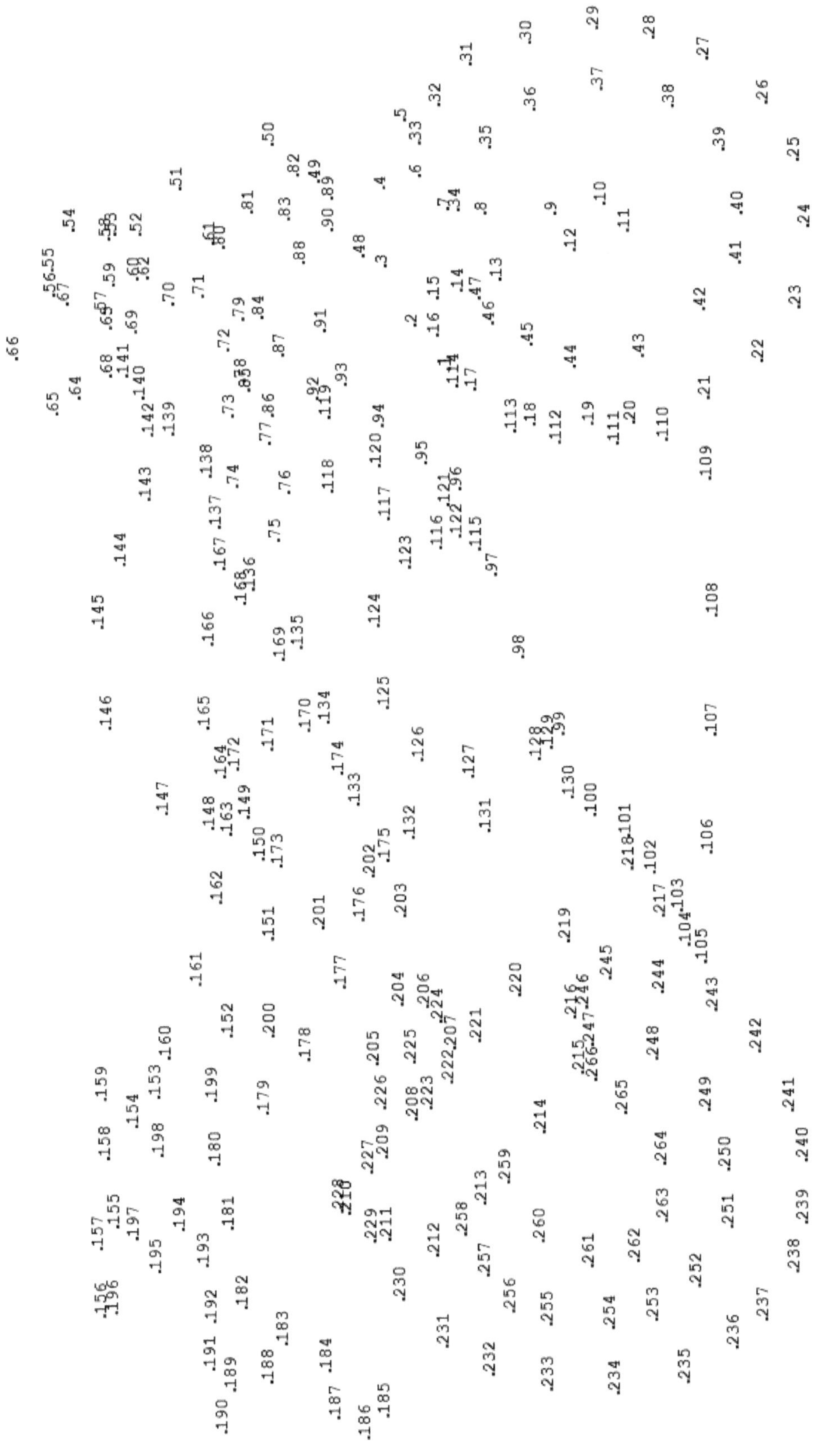

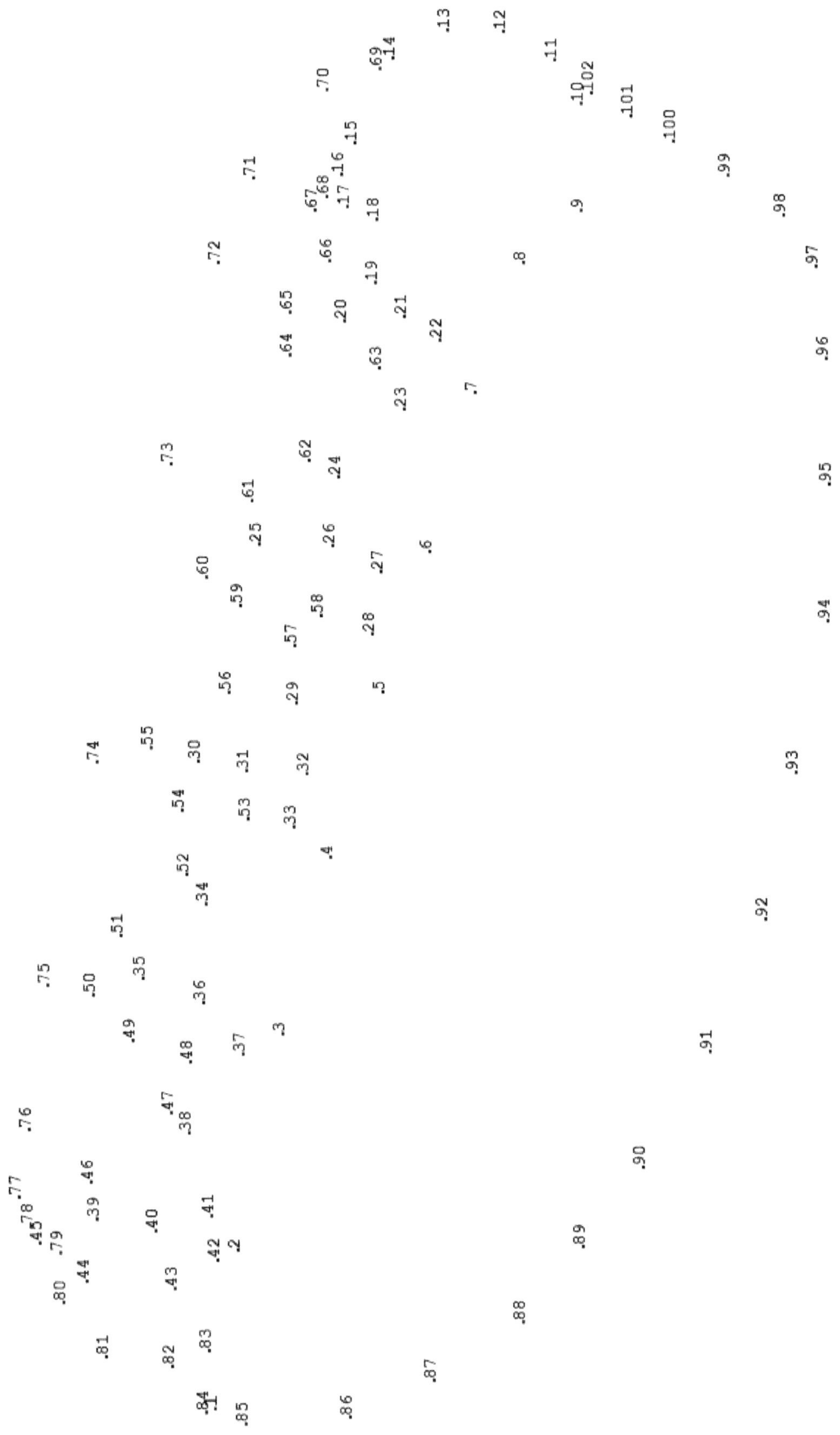

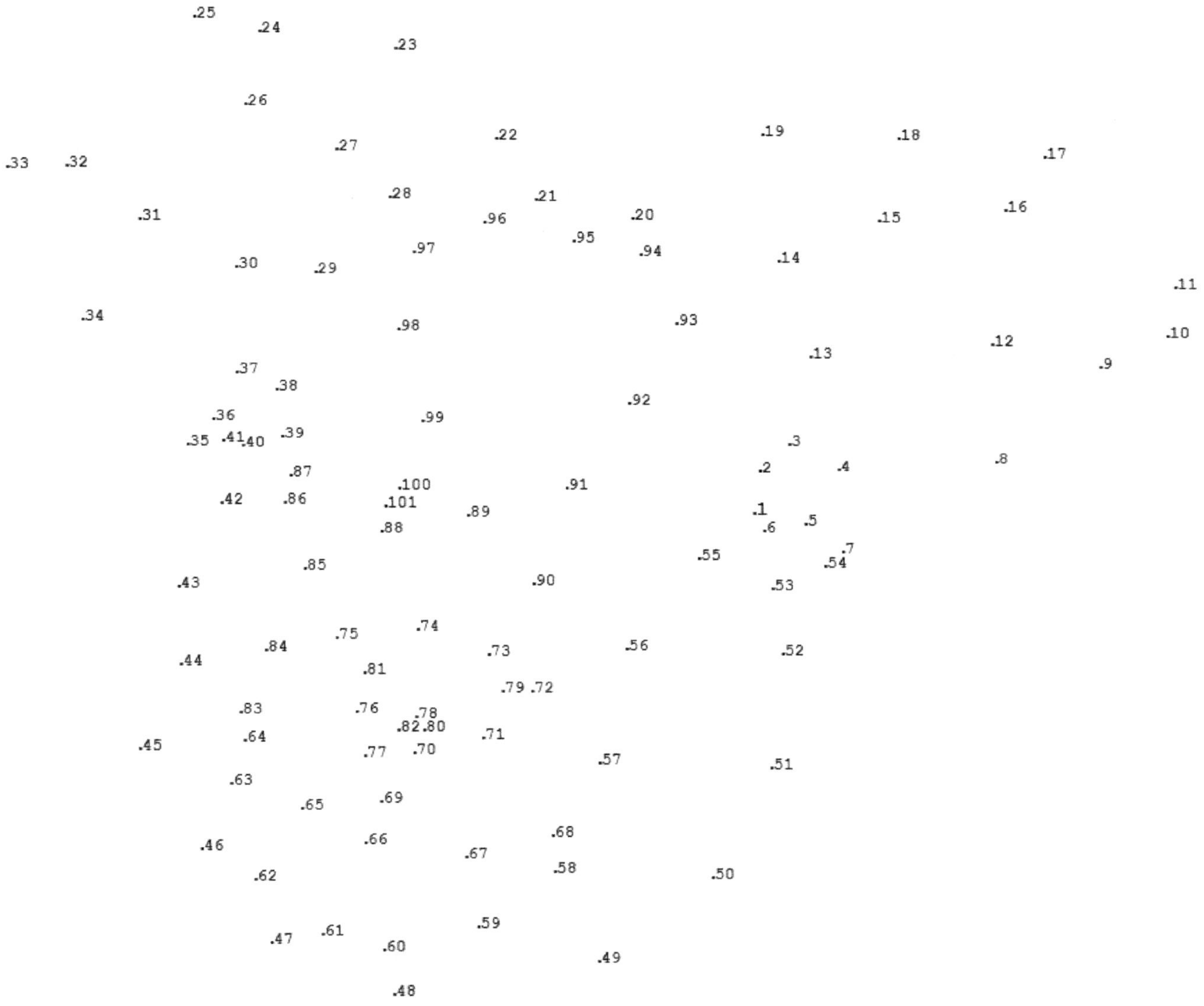
.1 .2 .3 .4 .5 .6 .7 .8 .9 .10
.11 .12 .13 .14 .15 .16 .17 .18 .19 .20
.21 .22 .23 .24 .25 .26 .27 .28 .29 .30
.31 .32 .33 .34 .35 .36 .37 .38 .39 .40
.41 .42 .43 .44 .45 .46 .47 .48 .49 .50
.51 .52 .53 .54 .55 .56 .57 .58 .59 .60
.61 .62 .63 .64 .65 .66 .67 .68 .69 .70
.71 .72 .73 .74 .75 .76 .77 .78 .79 .80
.81 .82 .83 .84 .85 .86 .87 .88 .89 .90
.91 .92 .93 .94 .95 .96 .97 .98 .99 .100
.101

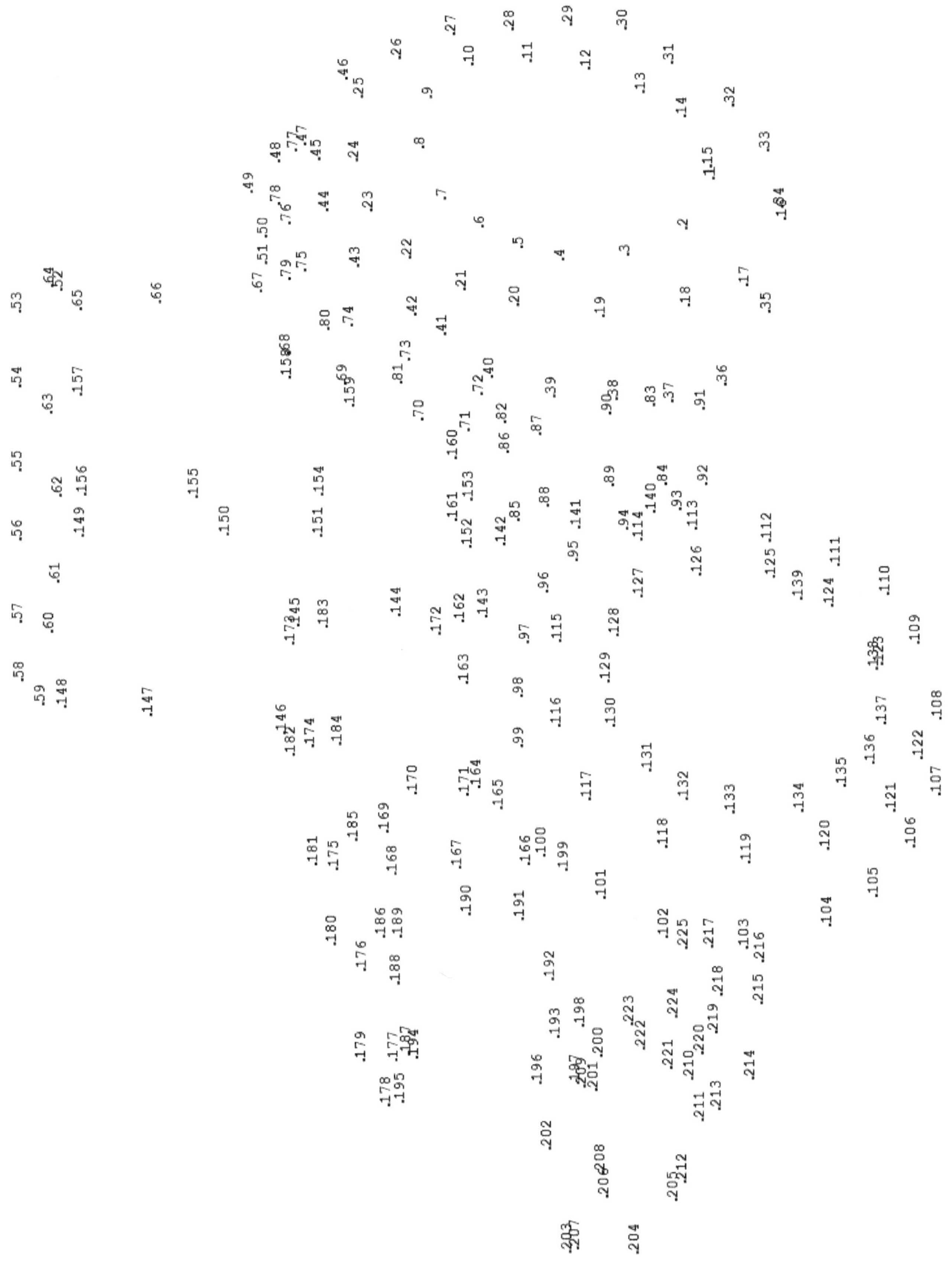

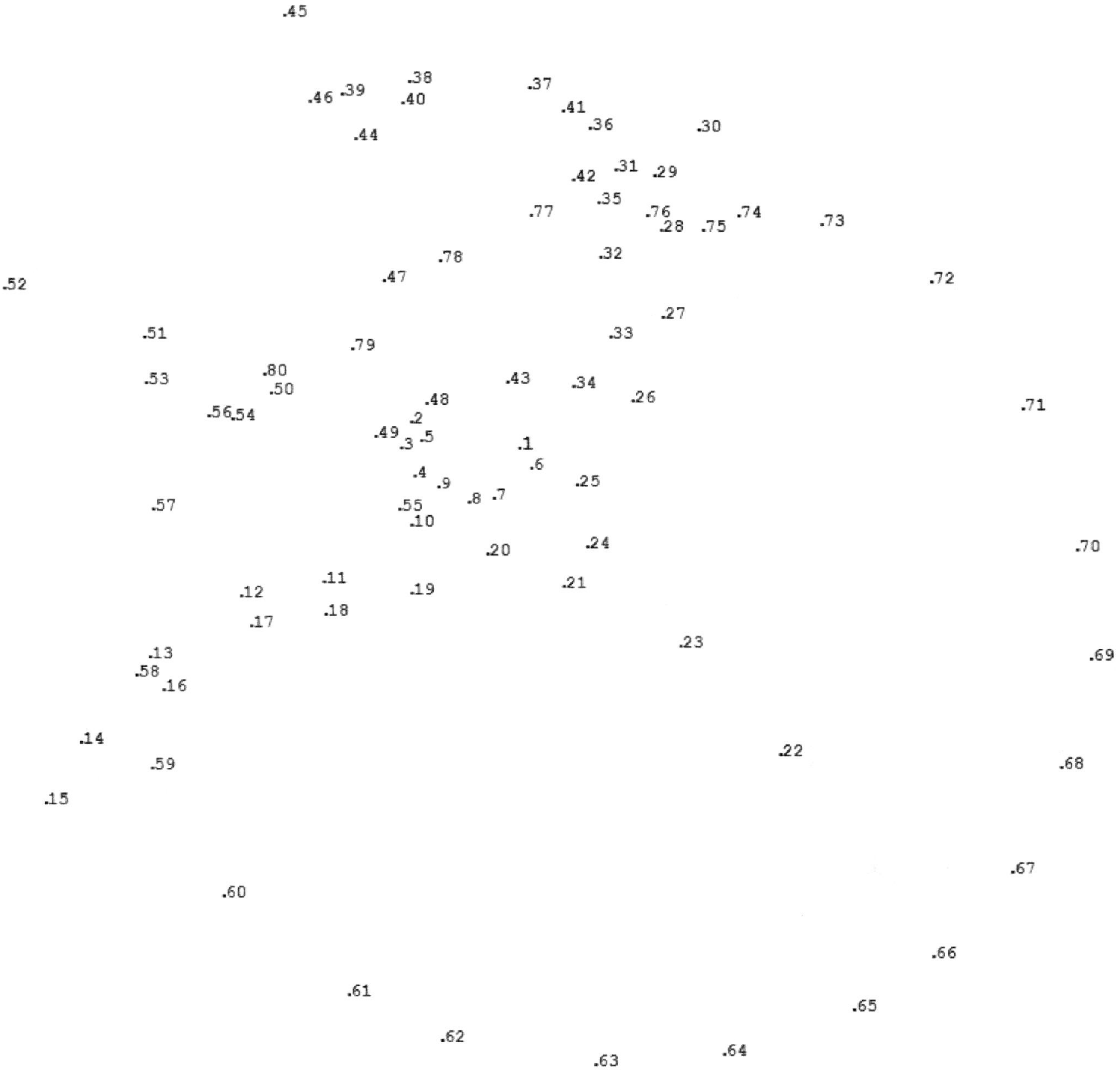
.1
.2
.3
.4
.5
.6
.7
.8
.9
.10
.11
.12
.13
.14
.15
.16
.17
.18
.19
.20
.21
.22
.23
.24
.25
.26
.27
.28
.29
.30
.31
.32
.33
.34
.35
.36
.37
.38
.39
.40
.41
.42
.43
.44
.45
.46
.47
.48
.49
.50
.51
.52
.53
.54
.55
.56
.57
.58
.59
.60
.61
.62
.63
.64
.65
.66
.67
.68
.69
.70
.71
.72
.73
.74
.75
.76
.77
.78
.79
.80

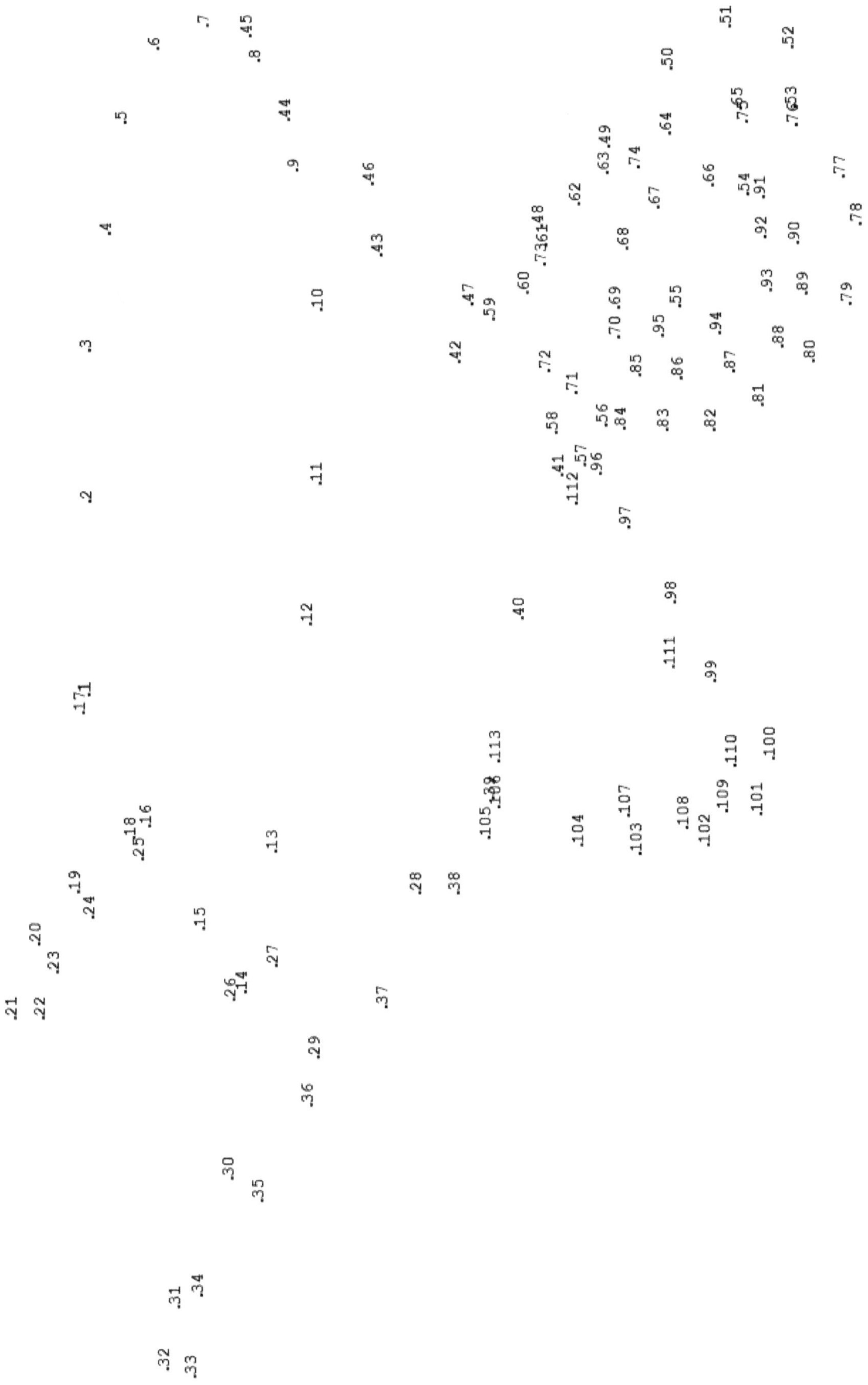

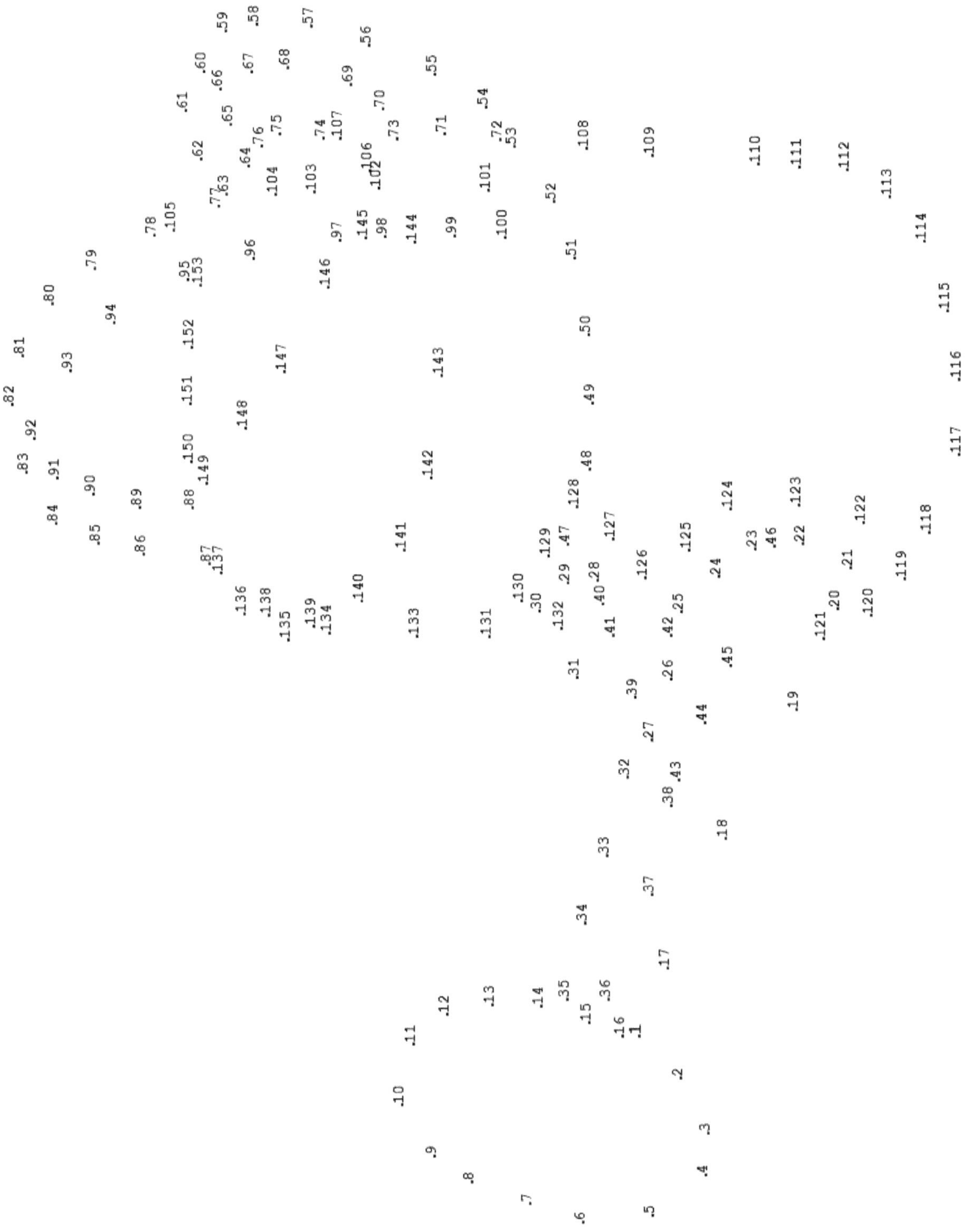

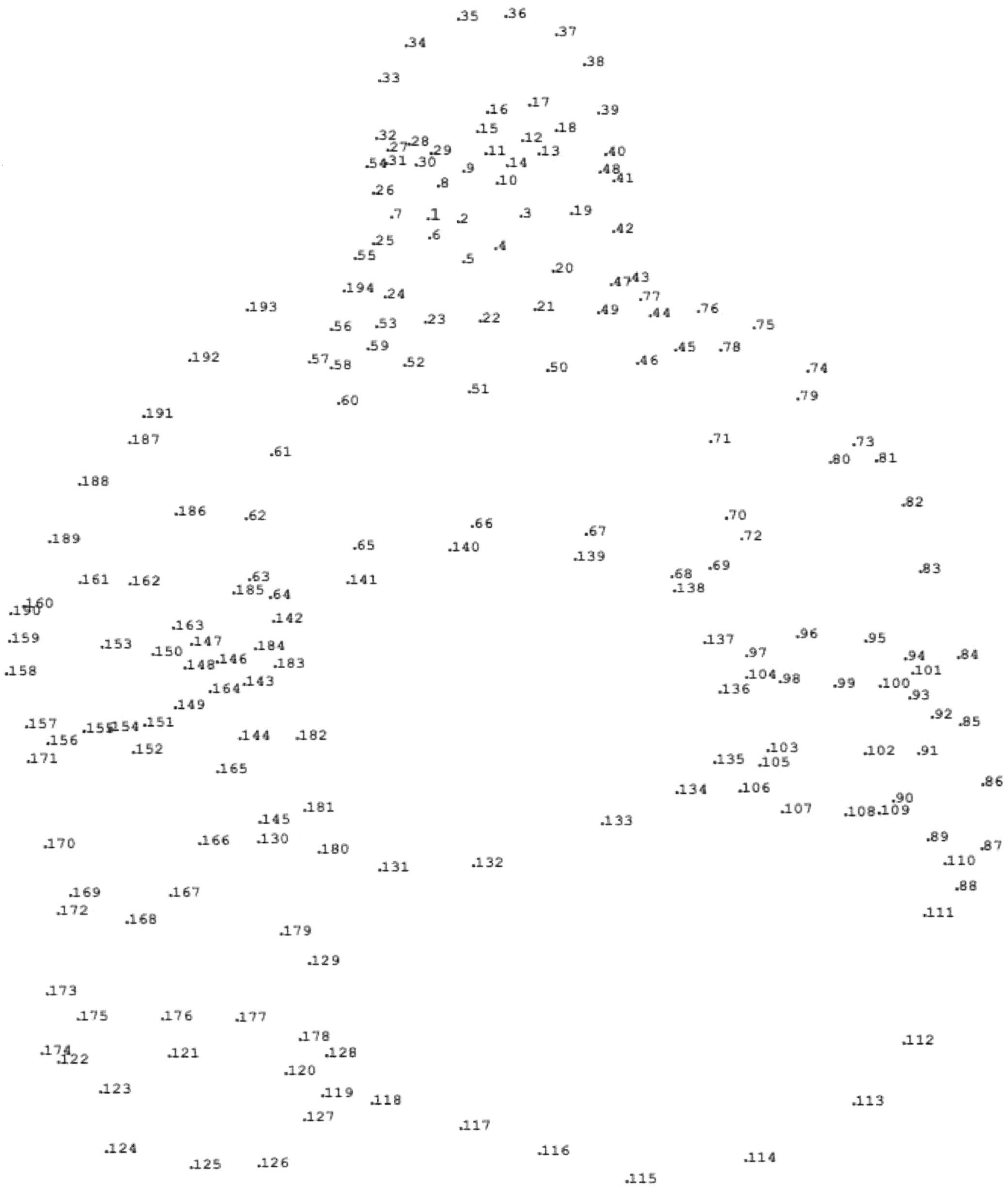

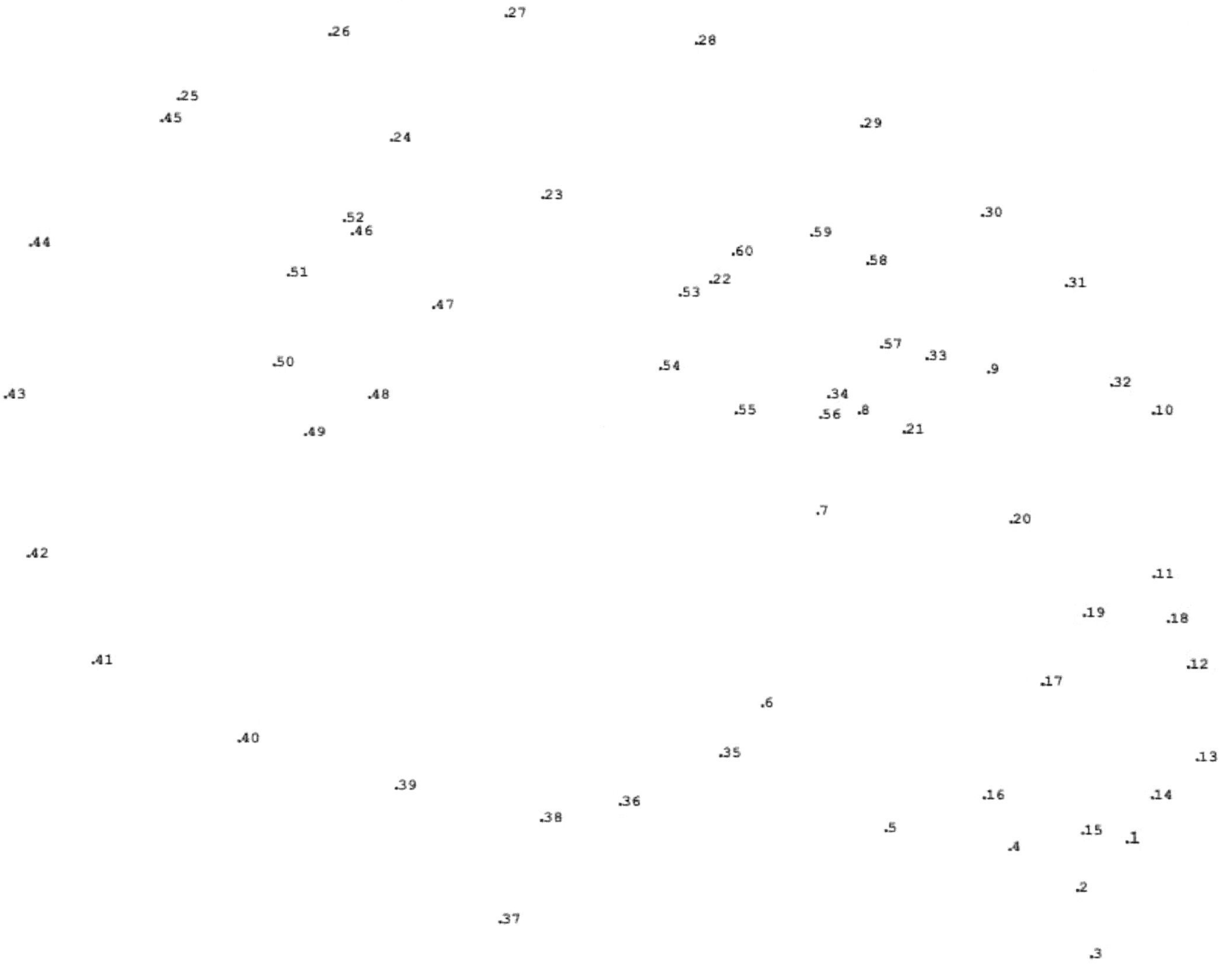

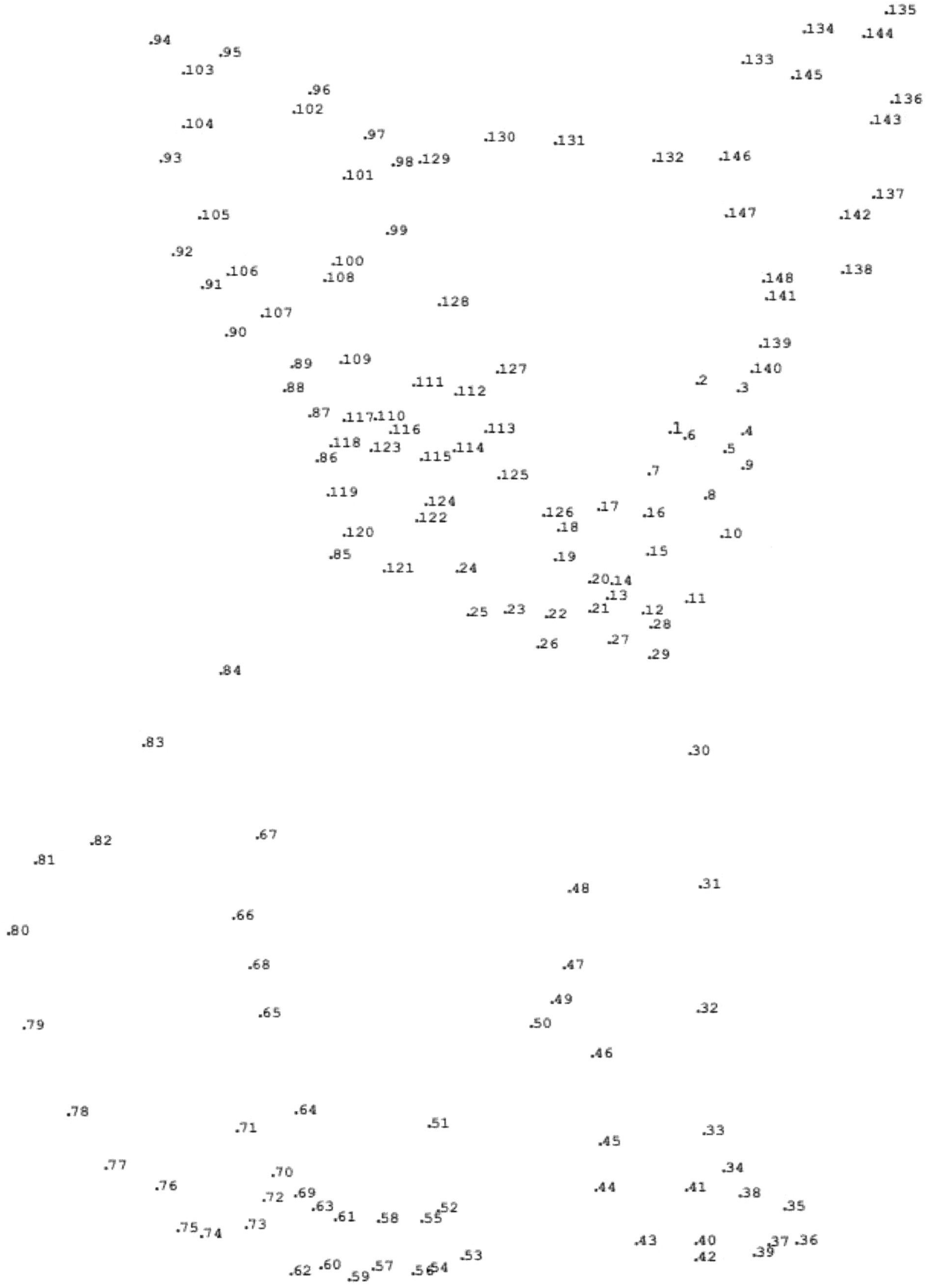

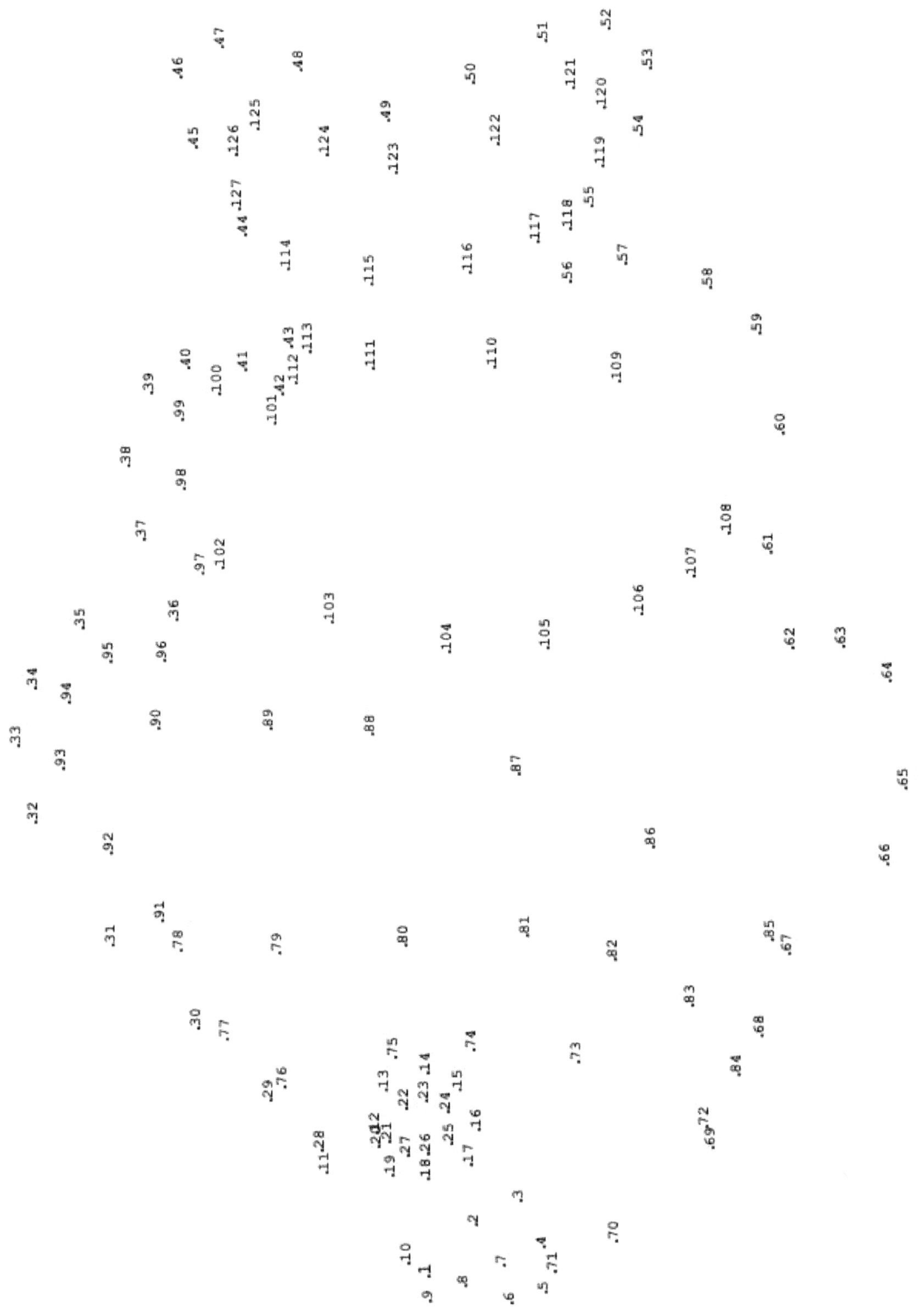

www.ingramcontent.com/pod-product-compliance
Lightning Source LLC
Chambersburg PA
CBHW080603220526
45466CB00010B/3232
9798592624452